Traditional Recipes of

OLD ENGLAND

Traditional Recipes of

OLD ENGLAND

Compiled by
Helen Edden

Illustrated by
Tony Burge

HIPPOCRENE BOOKS
New York

Originally published by Country Life, Ltd.

Hippocrene paperback edition, 1996.

For information, address:
HIPPOCRENE BOOKS, INC.
171 Madison Avenue
New York, NY 10016

Library of Congress Cataloging-in-Publication Data
Edden, Helen M.
        Traditional recipes of Old England / Helen Edden. --
Hippocrene pbk. ed.
                p.   cm.
        Originally published: London : Country Life, 1929.
        Includes index.
        ISBN 0-7818-0489-2
        1. Cookery, British. 2. Cookery--Great Britain. I. Title.
TX717.E42   1996   96-18958
641.5941--dc20   CIP

Printed in the United States of America.

Front cover artwork: Dining-Room of Cock Tavern , Fleet Street, by Philip Norman.

"To roast some beef, to carve a joint,
To boil up sauces, and to blow the fire,
Is anybody's task.   He who does this
Is but a seasoner and broth maker;
A cook is quite another thing.   His mind
Must comprehend all facts and circumstances:
Where is the place and what the time of supper;
Who are the guests and who are the entertainers,
What fish he ought to buy and where to buy it."

DIONYSIUS.

PREFACE

ALTHOUGH cookery books abound in a very great variety, I do not know of one which deals with the recipes of the dishes which are characteristic of the many parts of the United Kingdom, so I have collected these recipes of specialities from some very old cookery books in my possession, and have carefully edited them. Some of the recipes have been given to me by the country people and dwellers in those districts noted for some particular dish.

Though my book starts with the County dishes of England, my Scottish, Irish and Welsh friends, equally with my English friends, would feel aggrieved if National and other dishes not strictly of County origin were omitted. Such are, therefore, given in the second part of my book.

Some of the old-world dishes are very expensive, but I have inserted these on account of their interest; the majority of them are not expensive, and will be found pleasing to the palate, economical to the pocket, and a charming variety to the daily menu.

Whilst collecting these recipes I have come across many interesting details of the origin of some of the dishes, and also the customs in connection with their consumption. Everyone probably knows some of these customs, but few, if any, know them all. For instance, everyone is familiar with the custom of providing roast beef for Christmas, roast lamb for Easter, and a goose for Michaelmas, etc., but it is not so well known that the custom of bringing in the boar's head with much ceremony still survives at Oxford on Christmas Day, or that on Shrove Tuesday the pancake is still tossed in Westminster School.

Other customs prevail in different localities. In Cheshire, Herefordshire, and Lancashire, simnel cakes are a feature on Mothering Sunday in mid-Lent. In Yorkshire, on the ninth

Preface

of November, parkin is eaten and served with cups of hot milk whilst people are gathered around a blazing bonfire.

SCOTLAND has earned for herself the name of "The land of cakes," and of these Edinburgh shortbread, the popularity of which like porridge has spread to the South, may truly be described as the national cake.

IRELAND has its national dish of roast pig's face, which it served on all great occasions, and Bara Brith is the national bun loaf of Wales.

So I present this little book in the belief that it may prove of interest and of value to that large number of people who would like to prepare and cook the dainty and appetising dishes which have been proved to be excellent for so many years, and the like of which they may have enjoyed from time to time whilst away from home on holiday, or touring in the British Isles. To this end I have made the instructions as simple as possible, quite easy to understand, and if carefully carried out every dish must turn out a success.

CONTENTS

Contents

Traditional Recipes of

OLD ENGLAND

BERKSHIRE

BERKSHIRE BACON PUDDING

1 lb. of flour.
6 ozs. of suet.
6 ozs. of fat home-cured
Berkshire bacon.

2 onions.
A little sage.
Salt and pepper.

Shred the suet finely, mix with the flour, adding sufficient cold water to make a firm paste. Roll out as for a roly-poly. Then cover with thin pieces of the bacon. The onions must be very finely chopped and mixed with the sage and seasoning; this should be sprinkled over. Then roll up the pudding, close the ends tightly, wrap in a pudding cloth and boil for two hours.

BERKSHIRE CRITTEN PIES

½ lb. of lard scraps (crittens).
½ lb. of apples.
½ lb. of currants.
¼ lb. of moist sugar.

A little nutmeg.
1 lb. of flour.
½ lb. of lard.
A little baking powder.

Make a short crust with the flour and lard; chop up the apples and mix with the crittens, currants, sugar, and a little grated nutmeg. Line some saucers with the pastry, put in two tablespoonfuls of the mixture, cover with some more pastry, and crimp the edges. Bake in a moderate oven.

CAMBRIDGESHIRE

CREAM CHEESE, 1741

1 pint of milk.   1½ pints of cream.
                    Rennet.

Boil the cream, then put it to the new milk, and when blood warm put in a spoonful of rennet; when it is well come, take a large strainer, lay it in a great cheese fat, put the curd in gently upon the strainer, then lay it on the cheese board with a pound weight on the top. Let it drain three hours, then put the curd in a cheese cloth, smooth it over and put a weight on the top, turn every two hours, and next morning salt it and put it in a clean cloth.

SLIP COAT CHEESE, 1741

Take new milk and rennet quite cold, and when it is come, put it into the cheese fat and let it stand and whey for some time, then cover it and put a 2 lb. weight on it. When it holds together keep turning it for two or three days upon cheese fats till it is dry, then lay it on dock leaves or nettles, shifting the leaves often. In Cambridge the cheese is sold laid on small rushes.

in Cambridge

CHESHIRE

CHESTER BUNS

4 ozs. of butter.
2 lbs. of flour.
2 ozs. of castor sugar.

1 egg.
½ pint of condensed milk.
¼ pint of yeast.

Salt.

Rub the butter into the flour, which should be sifted, into which the castor sugar and a pinch of salt has been previously mixed. Warm the condensed milk and beat an egg into it, add the yeast, mix into a dough, and set to rise. When ready make into buns, put on to a greased tin to prove, bake about twenty minutes. Wash over with sugar and water.

CHESTER CAKE

¼ lb. of flour.
½ oz. of baking powder.
½ lb. of stale cake.

6 ozs. of treacle or golden syrup.
A few currants.
A little ground ginger.

Make some short paste and line the bottom of a Yorkshire pudding tin, and leave sufficient paste for a covering for the top. Spread this mixture over the paste in the tin, pass the flour and baking powder through a sieve into a basin, add the stale cake crumbled up finely, and a few currants and a little ground ginger. Mix with treacle or golden syrup, making a rather stiff mixture. Spread this evenly and cover with the remaining pastry. Brush it all over with egg and milk and mark it in small squares. Bake in a quick oven, and when cold divide with a sharp knife into the squares indicated.

CHESTER PUDDING

¼ lb. of flour.
4 ozs. of breadcrumbs.
4 ozs. of suet finely chopped.
2 ozs. of castor sugar.

¼ lb. of black currant jam.
1 small teaspoonful of bicarbonate of soda.
A little salt.

Mix the flour, suet, sugar, salt and breadcrumbs thoroughly in a basin. Make a well in the centre and put in the jam. Warm the milk and dissolve the soda in it; pour this on the top of the jam and mix everything together. Put in a well-greased mould or basin, cover with buttered paper, and steam for three hours. Serve with jam sauce.

BLACK CURRANT SAUCE

½ pint of cold water.   4 large tablespoonfuls of jam.
4 ozs. of loaf sugar.

Put all into a stewpan and boil rapidly for ten minutes. Pour it round the pudding, through a conical strainer; it should form a clear syrup.

CHESHIRE PORK PYE, 1765

Take a loin of pork, skin it, cut it into steaks, season it with salt, nutmeg and pepper. Make a good crust. Lay a layer of pork, then a large layer of pippins pared and cored, a little sugar enough to sweeten the pie, then another of pork; put in ½ pint of white wine, lay some butter on the top, and close your pie. If your pie be very large it will take 1 pint of white wine.

CORNWALL

CORNISH PASTIES

CORNWALL has a number of dishes peculiar to itself. Perhaps the best known is the pasty, which can be filled with a variety of ingredients, besides the usual beef, potato and onion. For instance, bacon and leeks are sometimes substituted, or fish and potato, turnips and ham, etc. The Cornish people often make a small opening in the top of the crust when the pasty is cooked and pour in a little thin cream. These pasties may be eaten hot or cold. The ordinary filling is in the following proportions:

$\frac{1}{2}$ lb. of beef.   1 onion.
$\frac{1}{4}$ lb. of potatoes.   Pepper and salt.
                    1 tablespoonful of water.

Chop the ingredients finely, season, and mix with the water to moisten. Use about a tablespoonful of the mixture for each pasty.

LEEKIE PASTY

3 leeks.   A few breadcrumbs.
3 small rashers of bacon.   1 tablespoonful of milk.
                    Pepper and salt.

Parboil the leeks, drain, and cut them in very thin slices; add the bacon cut up small; then mix with the crumbs, milk and seasoning.

leekie pasty

SHORT CRUST FOR THE PASTIES

1 lb. of flour.	6 ozs. of lard or dripping
1 teaspoonful of baking powder.	

Rub the lard into the flour until it is as fine as breadcrumbs; add the baking powder, and mix gradually with just sufficient water to form a smooth stiff paste. Roll this out once, and cut out rounds 4 in. in diameter. Place a tablespoonful of the mixture in the centre of each round. Beat an egg on a plate, and brush around the edges of each; then press the edges firmly together and form into a frill on the top. Brush all over with egg, and put into a quick oven for twenty minutes or half an hour.

SQUAB PIE

2 lbs. of apples.	2 ozs. of raisins,
2 ozs. of moist sugar.	A little mixed spice.
¼ lb. of cold mutton.	¼ pint of water.

Peel, core and slice the apples. Chop the mutton finely (it should be as lean as possible). Stone and chop the raisins. Then mix all the ingredients together and fill a pie dish. Cover with short crust, using the same recipe as for Cornish pasties, and bake in the oven until the apples are well cooked.

SAFFRON CAKE

1 lb. of dough.	2 ozs. of currants.
½d. worth of saffron.	1 oz. of candied peel.
2 ozs. of castor sugar.	3 ozs. of butter.
3 ozs. of lard.	

Make the dough in the ordinary way as for bread, but infuse the saffron in the warm water first to make it yellow. When the dough has risen, mix in the currants, sugar and candied peel, and, lastly, melt together the butter and lard. (This must not

mix in the currants

be made too hot, neither must it oil.) Pour on to the dough cake mixture, and beat it well in. Then knead well, and bake in a cake tin the same as for bread, letting the mixture rise to the top of the tin before placing it in the oven.

A CORNISH PASTRY RECIPE FOR MEAT PIES

1 lb. of flour.	¼ lb. of lard.
¼ lb. of suet.	A pinch of salt.

Flake the suet finely, then mix with the flour and salt, and make into a stiff paste with some cold water. Roll out and add the lard as for flaky pastry, in small lumps. Roll out again, until the whole is used. Let the pastry stand for a while. It is then ready for covering the pies.

BLACK CAKE

1 lb. of flour.	¼ lb. of chopped raisins (seeds
1 lb. of moist sugar.	removed).
¾ lb. of butter.	2 ozs. of sweet almonds, shredded.
¼ lb. of candied peel.	1 teaspoonful of bicarbonate of soda
1 lb. of currants.	6 eggs.

Cream the sugar and butter, mix the soda and flour together, and add the fruit, peel and almonds. Beat up the eggs and add these last. Bake in a slow oven.

SPLITS

1 lb. of flour.	1 oz. of butter.
½ oz. of yeast.	½ pint of skim milk.
1 teaspoonful of castor sugar.	A little salt.

Add the salt to the flour, mix the yeast with the sugar, dissolve the butter in the milk, and when this is tepid pour it on the yeast; then mix the flour to a dough. Let it stand in a

splits

warm place until well risen; then knead and shape into rounds about ½ in. thick. Brush them over with milk, and bake for fifteen minutes. Cut through, spread with plenty of butter or clotted cream, and serve hot.

FISH PIE

3 to 6 fresh herrings or mackerel.   A little butter.
Breadcrumbs, parsley, cayenne   Pastry to cover the pie.
and salt.

Wash, scale, and clean the fish and remove the bones. Lay the fish flat on the chopping board, and season the inside of each with salt, cayenne and parsley. Roll each one up. Grease a pie dish, put in a thick layer of breadcrumbs, then lay in some of the rolled fish, then breadcrumbs, and then more fish and crumbs. On the top put a few thin slices of bacon or ham. Pour over this about a gill of cream with a dash of tarragon vinegar. Cover the dish with pastry and bake; first arranging the heads in the centre of the pastry. This pie takes about an hour and a half to bake. Serve it hot and place a sprig of parsley in the mouth of each fish.

LEEK AND PILCHARD PIE

Some large leeks.   ½ pint of scalded cream.
Salted pilchards.   Good plain pastry to cover the pie.

Take just the white part of some large leeks, clean and skin them, then scald in milk and water, and slice them. Soak the pilchards for some hours the days before. Put alternate layers of pilchards and leeks into a pie dish, and cover with the pastry. When cooked, lift up the crust with a knife at one side and drain off all the liquor. Pour in the scalded cream and serve.

the liquor

CONGER EEL PIE

Fillet a conger eel by taking the flesh from each side of the bone, cut into 4 in. lengths, season with pepper and salt and a little finely chopped parsley. Roll up each piece, and place them in a pie dish until it is full. Add $\frac{1}{4}$ pint of veal broth, and cover the pie with some rough puff paste, brushed over with egg and ornamented on the top. Bake for an hour, and whilst the pie is baking make a sauce as follows: Boil all the trimmings of the fish (seasoned with salt and pepper) in $\frac{1}{2}$ pint of veal broth. Strain, thicken with a little flour and butter and a tablespoonful of lemon juice. Pour this boiling hot into the pie, making a hole in the centre for the purpose, and serve immediately.

KETTLE BROTH

This is a Cornish remedy for people suffering from colds. It is made by toasting a slice of bread, cutting it up into dice, and placing it in a basin with a small onion just peeled and left whole. Season with pepper and salt, and pour over $\frac{3}{4}$ pint of boiling water. Cover with a plate, let it stand for a few minutes, then remove the onion and serve.

STEWED WATERCRESSES

Wash the watercress well in strong salt and water, and pick off any dead leaves. Boil in water for about fifteen minutes, then drain well and chop up finely. Put a little butter in a stewpan, make hot, add the chopped cresses, season with pepper and salt, cook gently until quite tender, and add a teaspoonful of vinegar just before serving. This is very nice to serve with boiled chicken.

B

suffering from colds

CUMBERLAND

CUMBERLAND CURRANT CAKE

MAKE short pastry as in apple cake, but roll it out into an oblong strip about 10 by 20 ins. and cut strip into two 10-in. squares. Spread one square with washed currants, which are left wet, add a little finely cut candied peel and a dash of mixed spice. Sprinkle with sugar, moisten the edges with water, and cover with the second square of pastry. Lightly press with rolling pin, prick with a fork, and bake on a greased tin in a hot oven. When cool cut in small squares.

APPLE OR GOOSEBERRY CAKE

Make short pastry using ½ lb. of butter or lard to 1 lb. of flour. Roll out thinly. Cut rounds the size of a dinner plate. Put a round of pastry on a greased tin or iron oven shelf. On it spread a layer of sliced apples or gooseberries. Sprinkle with sugar and then lightly dust with flour to prevent the juice boiling out. Moisten the edges of the pastry and cover with a second round. Crimp the edges and bake in a hot oven. Allow to cool and then dust with icing sugar and put on a plate. Serve cold.

RUM BUTTER

A dish of rum butter is always made when there has been a birth in Cumberland. Visitors to the house are given a glass of wine, in which to drink the health of the new arrival, and with this wine they eat arrowroot biscuits spread with rum butter.

1 lb. of butter.	3 ozs. of rum.
1 lb. of brown sugar.	A little nutmeg.

a birth in Cumberland

Warm butter and sugar in a basin. Beat to a cream and add rum and nutmeg. Beat again and put into glass dishes such as lunch tongues are sold in. Smooth the top with a knife and serve like jam.

MUTTON PIES

Cut into small pieces 1 lb. of lean mutton. Line some deep patty tins with short pastry. Fill with the mutton. Add a little chopped onion and chopped parsley to each. Cover with well-seasoned gravy to which a little ketchup has been added. Cover with rounds of pastry, and crimp edges. Make a hole in each with a skewer, and cook in a moderate oven for about an hour. Remove pies from tins and serve garnished with parsley.

ALMOND PUDDINGS

2 ozs. of butter.	4 ozs. of rice flour.
2 ozs. of castor sugar.	2 tablespoonfuls of ground
2 eggs.	almonds.

Raspberry jam.

Line three saucers with short pastry and prick with fork. Spread with thin layer of raspberry jam. Beat the butter and castor sugar to a cream, add the eggs and work in the rice flour and ground almonds. Spread this over the jam and bake in a moderate oven. Serve hot.

SAND CAKE

2 ozs. of butter.	1 teaspoonful of baking
4 ozs. of castor sugar.	powder.
4 ozs. of cornflour.	2 eggs.
1 oz. of plain flour.	Few drops of essence of lemon.

Beat butter and sugar to a cream. Add eggs and the cornflour, plain flour, and baking powder. Mix thoroughly and bake in a well-greased and lined cake tin.

VANILLA JELLY

2 tablespoonfuls of sugar.   1 pint of milk.

2 eggs.   Few drops of vanilla essence.

½ oz. of powdered gelatine.

Warm the milk and add the yolks of the eggs beaten with the sugar and a few drops of vanilla essence. Stir over gentle heat until creamy. Pour into a basin. Dissolve the powdered gelatine in a tablespoonful of water in the saucepan. Add this to contents of basin, and lastly stir in lightly the stiffly beaten whites of the two eggs. Pour into a wetted mould and allow to set. Turn out.

SPARE-RIB PIE

Cut up 2 lbs. of spare rib of pork and arrange it in a deep pie dish. Season with pepper and salt and chopped parsley. Half fill dish with cold water. Cover with a thick crust of good short pastry. Ornament with leaves of pastry. Make a hole in the top and bake in a steady oven for one and a half hours. Serve cold with pickled beetroot.

ornament with leaves

DERBYSHIRE

BAKEWELL TART

Puff pastry.	¼ lb. of butter.
Raspberry and currant jam.	2 eggs.
¼ lb. of sugar.	4½ ozs. of flour.

Line some saucers with puff paste, and put in a layer of jam. Cream the butter and sugar together; beat in one egg and then half the flour, then the second egg and the rest of the flour. Spread this mixture over the jam, covering it right to the edge. Bake until the pastry is a light fawn colour.

DERBY CAKES

¼ lb. of butter.	¼ lb. of moist sugar.
1 lb. of flour.	1 egg.
½ lb. of currants.	¼ pint of milk.

Rub the butter lightly into the flour, then add the sugar and the currants. Mix with the egg and milk, form into a paste and roll it out thin, and cut into little round cakes with a cutter. Lay them on a buttered baking sheet, and bake them slowly for about ten minutes.

SAVOURY PUDDING
(To Eat with Pork or Goose)

1 teacupful of fine oatmeal.	1 pint of milk.
2 teacupfuls of breadcrumbs.	1 lb. of onions very finely chopped.
2 teacupfuls of flour.	
¼ lb. of suet, finely chopped.	1 teaspoonful of chopped sage.
2 eggs.	Pepper and salt to season.

or goose

Make the milk hot, and pour it over the breadcrumbs and oatmeal. Let it stand for ten minutes, then beat in the two eggs. Mix the seasoning with the flour, add the onions, and mix thoroughly. Bake for about one hour, and serve in the same manner as a Yorkshire pudding.

serve in the same manner
as a Yorkshire pudding

DEVONSHIRE

BOILED APPLE DUMPLINGS

1 lb. of suet crust.	8 cloves.
8 apples.	Some moist sugar.

Choose good baking apples of about equal size, pare them thinly, and take out the core with a cutter. Roll out the pastry to about ⅛ in. thick and cut out sixteen rounds, so that each round will cover half an apple. Then fill the centre of the apple with moist sugar and one clove. Moisten the edge of the paste with a little water, put another round of paste on top, and join the edges neatly. Tie the dumplings securely in well-floured pudding cloths (allowing room to rise), and boil them for one hour. When cooked remove the cloths and send quickly to table.

For the suet crust the ingredients are: 1 lb. of flour, 6 oz. of suet, 1 teaspoonful of baking powder. Shred and chop the suet finely, put it into a basin, and pass the flour and baking powder through a sieve on to it. Mix all to a stiff smooth paste with a little cold water and roll out once. For a richer crust use ½ lb. of suet.

DEVONSHIRE JUNKET

1 quart of new milk.	A little grated nutmeg.
1 dessertspoonful of essence of rennet.	Clotted cream.
1 tablespoonful of best brandy.	1 tablespoonful of castor sugar.

Mix the milk, brandy and sugar together, and warm in a white saucepan to a temperature of 100°—not more. Pour into a china bowl or glass dish, add the rennet, stirring gently but thoroughly a few times, and allow to set. The junket should then be smooth, shiny and firm. Grate a little nutmeg over the top, and dot about small lumps of clotted cream.

DEVONSHIRE CREAM

Pour into a large shallow pan two gallons of milk, which must be quite fresh. Allow it to stand for about six hours, until the cream rises, then place it on the cool end of a closed kitchener, or over a tiny glimmer of gas on a long burner, and let the milk very, very slowly get thoroughly hot. It should take quite an hour, and the milk must on no account be allowed to boil, or it will spoil the richness and texture of the cream. Remove, and allow to cool for a whole day before removing the cream.

EXETER STEW

1½ lbs. of beef steak.	1 tablespoonful of flour (mixed
2 carrots.	with a little salt and pepper).
2 turnips.	1½ pints of stock.
2 onions.	2 ozs. of butter.

Cut the steak into small pieces, and fry it in the butter with the onions chopped small. Cook for five minutes, then sprinkle over the flour and seasoning, add the stock gradually, and, when it boils, the carrots and turnips in thin pieces. Simmer gently for two hours. Then put in about six or eight small savoury dumplings, and cook for half an hour longer. Put the meat in the centre of a dish with the vegetables, and garnish with the dumplings.

For the dumplings the ingredients are: 6 tablespoonfuls of flour, ¼ teaspoonful of baking powder, 3 ozs. of finely shredded and chopped suet, about ¼ pint of water, 1 dessertspoonful of chopped parsley, a pinch of sweet herbs, and a pinch of salt. Put the suet into the flour, add all the dry ingredients, and use the water to make into a smooth dough. Divide into tiny balls without cracks, and free from dry flour.

EVERTON TOFFEE

1 lb. of sugar.   6 ozs. of butter.
½ gill of milk.

Put all the ingredients into a saucepan and boil gently for
about twenty minutes. Try a little upon a cold plate to see
if it will set. Allow it to stand until it ceases bubbling, then
pour into a hot buttered shallow tin. When half cold, mark
into squares; and when quite cold break and wrap in greaseproof paper. Keep in an airtight tin.

DEVON BREAKFAST DISH: LAMB'S FRY

Lamb's fry.   1 small onion.
A little parsley.   2 ozs. butter.
1 lemon.

Everton toffee

Wash and dry the fry, cut it up in small slices, and roll it in a
little flour seasoned with pepper and salt. Chop the onion
finely, and cook it in the butter until light brown, then add the
lamb's fry and cook gently for about ten minutes, until it is well
browned. Add a squeeze of lemon juice when it is dished,
sprinkle over some finely chopped parsley and serve very hot.

DEVON POTATO CAKE

6 ozs. of flour.   A pinch of mixed spice.
6 ozs. of well-boiled potatoes.   ½ oz. of carraway seeds.
¼ lb. of moist sugar.   2 eggs.
¼ lb. of currants.   2 ozs. of butter.
1 teaspoonful of baking powder.

Pass the potatoes through a sieve or potato masher, add the
flour and baking powder, and rub in the butter. Mix in all the
dry ingredients, and also the two eggs, well beaten. Bake
in a flat tin, well greased, in a fairly hot oven for half an hour.
This cake should be served hot for tea, cut up into squares.

DEVONSHIRE SQUAB PIE

2 lbs. of neck of mutton chops.   1 onion.
2 lbs. of sour apples.   Ground allspice, pepper, salt.
              Short pastry to cover.

Trim the chops and cut them short, removing a little of the fat if necessary. Peel, core, and slice the apples, and chop the onion finely. Fill a pie dish, putting in first a layer of meat, then one of onion and apples. Season well and repeat until the dish is full. Pour in ¼ pint of gravy or water and cover with the pastry. This pie will take about two hours to bake in a moderate oven and should be sent to table very hot.

DEVON CAKES

½ lb. of clotted cream.   1 egg.
1 lb. of flour.   ¼ lb. of sugar.
              A little milk.

Rub the cream into the flour, beat in the egg, add the sugar, and mix into a smooth paste, using a little milk if necessary to make it the consistency of dough. Roll out rather thin, and cut into small shapes. Sprinkle each with grated loaf sugar, and bake in a quick oven for about ten minutes.

GLOUCESTERSHIRE

GLOUCESTER CHEESE AND ALE

Cut some good Gloucester cheese into thin flakes, removing first any rind. Put these in a fireproof dish, spread some mustard over and cover with strong ale. Cook until quite tender and the cheese dissolved. Have ready some slices of thick brown toast. Pour hot ale over the toast sufficiently to moisten it, then the cheese, and serve very hot.

CHELTENHAM CAKES

2 lbs. of flour.	1 pint of warm milk.
¼ lb. of butter.	Yolks of 2 eggs.
½ teacupful of brewer's yeast.	

Melt the butter in the milk, then mix all the ingredients together, and set it to rise for an hour or so in a warm place. Make into round buns about the size of a small tea saucer. Let them rise again. Then bake in a sharp oven for about fifteen minutes.

— a sharp oven

HAMPSHIRE

ISLE OF WIGHT DOUGH NUTS

2 ozs. of butter.	Frying fat.
1 lb. of flour.	1 oz. of castor sugar.
½ oz. of yeast.	Jam (raspberry).
2 eggs.	1½ gills of warm milk.

Pinch of salt.

Divide the flour, salt and castor sugar into two basins, after well mixing and passing through a sieve. Into one rub the butter, into the other mix the yeast and milk. Let it rise for half-an-hour, then mix both together and beat in the two eggs. Now let it stand in a warm place for an hour to rise. Knead and divide into twenty-four pieces, shape each into a round ball, make a hole and insert a little jam in the centre; close up securely, using a little egg to moisten the edges. Let them stand on a floured tin for ten minutes to " prove." Drop them into a deep bath of boiling fat, only four or five at a time, until they obtain a golden brown colour. Drain on kitchen paper and roll in castor sugar.

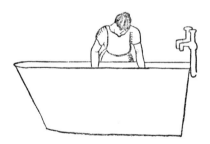

a deep bath

HUNTINGDONSHIRE

HUNTINGDON PUDDING

½ lb. of flour.   1 egg.
5 ozs. of suet.   A little baking powder.
3 ozs. of castor sugar.   ¼ pint of milk.
              1 pint of gooseberries.

Mix the flour, and the suet very finely chopped, together.
Then mix the baking powder with the castor sugar and add next.
Then the gooseberries, which should have been washed and
prepared. Stir all together. Beat up the egg in the milk,
and gradually mix. Steam in a greased basin covered with
buttered paper for three hours, and serve with a sweet sauce.

SWEET SAUCE

1 oz. of butter.   ½ pint of milk.
½ oz. of flour.   1 oz. of sugar.

Melt the butter and add the flour in the same method
as other sauces, then add the milk and sugar, and boil well,
stirring all the time. To vary the flavour, the rind of a lemon
or a bay leaf may be boiled in the milk. Strain round the
pudding.

KENT

KENTISH CHEESE PASTIES

1 lb. of flour.	¾ lb. of cheese cut in very
¼ lb. of butter.	thin flakes and mixed with
¼ lb. of lard.	little pieces of butter.
Cayenne and salt.	1 egg.

Make some flaky pastry with the flour, butter and lard. Roll out ⅛th in. thick, cut into rounds the size of a saucer. Place a tablespoonful of the flaked cheese and butter in the centre, and sprinkle over some cayenne and salt. Moisten the edges of the pastry and form into little pasties. Brush over with beaten egg. These should be served quite *hot*.

FOLKESTONE PUDDING PIES

1 lb. of flour.	½ oz. of ground rice.
3 ozs. of butter.	2 ozs. of currants.
3 ozs. of lard.	3 eggs.
1 pint of milk.	1 tablespoonful of sugar.

Make a short crust with the flour, butter and lard, and line some breakfast saucers—just marking the edges. Make ¾ pint of milk hot in a saucepan. Mix the ground rice and castor sugar together with the remainder of the milk, turn into the hot milk and stir until it thickens. Remove from the fire, allow to cool a little, and gradually mix in the eggs one at a time, stirring vigorously. Fill with this mixture, then sprinkle over a few currants. Bake to a golden brown.

HOT FLEAD CAKES

1 lb. of flour.
1 lb. of leaf or flear (called "flead" in Kent).

Pinch of salt.
½ pint of cold water to mix.
1 egg.

Sieve the flour and salt together. Scrape a little of the flead and rub lightly in. Mix into a dough with cold water, knead lightly, and roll out on a floured board. Scrape some more of the flead and spread it over the paste in flakes, fold, and beat out with the rolling pin. Repeat until the flead is all used. Then roll out to about ¼ in. thickness, and cut into small rounds, diamonds and slightly larger rounds, folded over. Brush over with egg, bake in a sharp oven to a golden brown, and eat hot. This pastry is also used in Kent for fruit and meat pies, turnovers, etc.

KENTISH WELL PUDDING

1 lb. of flour.
6 ozs. of suet.
6 ozs. of currants.

A little baking powder.
½ lb. of fresh farmhouse butter.

2 tablespoonfuls of moist sugar.

Make a suet crust with the flour, suet and currants, incorporated. Roll out 1½ ins. thick, and line a greased pudding basin. In the well place the ½ lb. of butter and fill up the crevices with the sugar. Cover with the rest of the pastry, joining the edges well. Cover with a greased paper and steam for three or four hours.

KENTISH RABBIT PUDDING

1 lb. of flour.
6 ozs. of suet.
A little baking powder.

1 wild rabbit.
½ lb. of pickled pork.
Salt and pepper to taste.

Make a suet crust and roll out into a round. Scald and flour a pudding cloth, spread it in a colander, and place the pastry

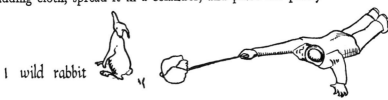

1 wild rabbit

in. The rabbit must be well washed and cut in tiny pieces with the pork in small slices, and seasoned with a sprinkling of flour, pepper and salt. Form the pudding into the shape of a globe. Tie up in the pudding cloth and boil for quite four hours.

KENTISH PUDDING PIE

3 ozs. of ground rice.	1 oz. of sugar.
1½ pints of milk.	2 eggs.
4 ozs. of butter.	Some pastry.

Boil the ground rice in the milk. Beat the butter to a cream, add the sugar, then beat in the eggs, one after the other. Now mix all with the ground rice and milk. Bake this mixture in a pie dish lined with short paste.

OAST CAKES FOR TEA

1 lb. of flour.	½ teacupful of sugar.
1 teaspoonful of baking powder.	4 ozs. of lard.
½ teaspoonful of salt.	6 ozs. of currants.

Put the dry ingredients into the bowl, rub in the lard, then add the currants. Mix into a light dough with water, adding a teaspoonful of lemon juice, and pinch off the pieces. Roll the pieces out lightly on the pasteboard, and fry to a golden brown in a little lard. They should be eaten hot from the pan.

TUNBRIDGE WELLS CAKES

½ lb. of flour.	4 ozs. of castor sugar.
2 ozs. of butter.	2 ozs. of carraway seeds.
A pinch of salt.	

Rub the butter into the flour, then add the rest of the ingredients and mix with a little cold water into a stiff paste. Work until smooth, then roll out very thin and stamp in small rounds. Prick on the surface with a fork and bake on a buttered baking sheet in a moderate oven about ten to fifteen minutes.

LANCASHIRE

MANCHESTER PUDDING

½ pint of milk.
The rind of 1 lemon.
2 ozs. of breadcrumbs.
1 oz. of castor sugar.

2 eggs.
2 ozs. of butter.
1 tablespoonful of brandy.
Jam and some puff paste.

Boil the lemon rind in the milk and pour this on to the breadcrumbs. Let it stand for five minutes, then remove the peel, beat in the yolks only of the eggs, the butter, sugar and brandy.

Line a pie dish with short crust and decorate the edge. Then put in a layer of any kind of stoneless jam. Cover with the breadcrumb mixture and bake gently for three-quarters of an hour. Whip up the whites stiffly with some castor sugar, and arrange smoothly on the top, then dredge a little more sugar over and put in the oven to set. Serve this pudding cold.

LANCASHIRE POTATO PIE

1 lb. of raw beef steak.
2 lbs. of potatoes.
¼ lb. of suet.

1 lb. of flour and a little
    baking powder.
Pepper and salt.

Cut the meat in pieces, cover with cold water and stew gently until tender. Put this into a pie dish with the gravy and season well. Peel, wash, and slice the potatoes, and fill up the pie dish. Cover with a suet crust and bake for one hour.

c

decorate the edge

LANCASHIRE HOT POT

Lancashire is reputed to be the birthplace of the hot pot. An earthenware " pipkin " is recommended for it, but, of course, a casserole will do the same work, as slow cooking under a close cover is the object to be attained.

The essential ingredients are chops of the very best mutton, mushrooms and kidneys; a suspicion of ham flavouring and a touch of red pepper.   Here is the recipe.

2 lbs. of chops.	2 lbs. of potatoes.
3 sheep's kidneys.	1 lb. of onions.
¼ lb. of mushrooms.	½ pint of stock.
2 ozs. of butter.	Pepper and salt, and cayenne.
2 ozs. of ham.	

Trim the chops, skin the kidneys, and cut them into rounds about ¼ in. thick.   Peel and slice the onions and potatoes and chop the ham finely.   Then arrange everything in layers in the pot, first meat, then kidneys, mushrooms, ham, onions and potatoes, sprinkling some pepper and salt over.   The last layer must be potatoes.   Pour over the stock and put the butter in small pieces on the top.   Cover with the lid closely and cook in the oven *very* slowly for about three hours.   Then remove the lid and allow the top to take a nice rich brown colour. This dish should be sent to table in the pot.

ECCLES CAKES

These cakes are peculiar to Lancashire.   The ingredients are:

Short crust pastry.	Currants.
Golden syrup.	Desiccated cocoanut.

Line some patty pans with short crust, put into each a layer of syrup, then currants and then the cocoanut.   Cover over with pastry and bake, or line a baking tin with the pastry.   Put the mixture over in layers and cover with more pastry. Just mark in finger-shaped pieces, and bake. When cold, cut up into pieces.

Note:—The above mixture would be greatly improved by adding 1 oz. of ground almonds, a little nutmeg and mace, with a few drops of lemon juice.

LANCASHIRE BUN LOAF

2 lbs. of bread dough.	½ lb. of currants.
¼ lb. of butter.	2 ozs. of orange peel.
½ lb. of stoned raisins.	½ oz. of mixed spice.

Place the dough on to a board and work into it first the butter (just melted), then the fruit and spice, the raisins stoned, the currants carefully cleaned and picked, and the orange peel chopped small. Knead till all is thoroughly mixed in with the dough.

Put the cake into a large buttered tin and allow it to stand in a warm place covered with a cloth to prove for quite an hour. When well risen, bake in a quick oven the same as for bread.

SIMNEL CAKES

These cakes are always made for the fourth Sunday in Lent— in many counties, but principally in Lancashire. In olden days it was the custom for families to meet on this Sunday that they might worship together in their Mother Church, and it was made the occasion also for a home festival in honour of the mothers. Sons and daughters went " a-mothering " with gifts of flowers and cake, and the cake was intended to be eaten whilst the whole family were present. Tradition says that the cakes took the name of Simnel from a couple who could not agree whether to have a plum cake or an almond one, so they finally decided to combine the two. Their names were Simon and Nellie; hence the name of Simnel, a combination of the two ! These cakes have always a layer of almond paste in the centre, and around the top.

a couple who could not agree

One recipe for the cake mixture is as follows:

¼ lb. of butter.	¼ lb. of currants.
¼ lb. of white sugar.	2 ozs. of candied peel.
¼ lb. of flour.	2 eggs.

Work the butter to a cream, then add the sugar and eggs (well beaten), then the flour, and lastly the fruit.

For the almond paste (which should be mixed before the cake mixture) the ingredients are:

¼ lb. ground sweet almonds;
¼ lb. brown sugar; and
2 eggs—

mixed well together

Put half the cake mixture into a tin, then a layer of almond paste. Fill the tin with the remainder of this cake mixture, and bake one and a half to two hours. When sufficiently baked place the remaining portion of the almond paste on the top, in small balls, on a plain rim. Put back in the oven until set.

Another recipe for simnel cake is as follows:

For the cake mixture—

2 ozs. each of butter, sugar and flour.	4 eggs.
¼ lb. of mixed peel.	Grated nutmeg, allspice, cinnamon, mace, ginger.
¼ lb. of raisins.	1 wineglassful of brandy or rum.
¼ lb. of currants.	
¼ lb. of ground almonds.	

For the almond paste—

½ lb. of ground almonds.	1 egg.
¼ lb. of brown sugar.	1 oz. of bitter ground almonds.
1 tablespoonful of brandy.	

Half of the cake mixture should be put in a buttered tin, lined with buttered paper, then put a layer of almond icing, and the rest of the cake mixture over it.   Spread this smoothly, and put the remainder of the almond icing on the top of the cake.

ORMSKIRK BRAWN—A BREAKFAST DISH

Take a pig's head, split it open, remove the brains, sprinkle thickly with salt and let it lie for twelve hours.   Then rub it well with 1½ ozs. of saltpetre and 6 ozs. of moist sugar.   Put into a pickle made of 1 lb. bay salt boiled in 4 quarts of water, and allowed to get cold.   Turn it every day for four days.

Take up the head, wash it, and divide it as much as possible. Put it on to boil in some clear spring water, with 1½ lbs. of beef— only just sufficient water to cover.   Skin well and cook until the meat leaves the bones.   Strain and cut up all the meat quickly into dice. Season with salt, black pepper, cayenne, and a little grated nutmeg.   Then return the stock to the saucepan, put in the meat, let it boil up well, and pour into wetted moulds.   Turn out when cold and serve.

OLDHAM PARKIN CAKE

14 ozs. of flour.	¼ oz. of ground mace.
8 ozs. of fine oatmeal.	1½ ozs. of candied lemon peel.
¼ lb. of butter.	¼ of small nutmeg grated.
¼ lb. of sugar.	1 teaspoonful of carbonate of
¼ oz. of ground ginger.	soda.

Rub the butter into the mixed flour and oatmeal, shred and chop finely the candied peel, then add the flavouring of ginger and nutmeg, with the sugar and soda.   Warm 14 ozs. of treacle in a little saucepan, add to it a large tablespoonful of cream, and pour on to the dry ingredients. Let the mixture stand all night.   In the morning bake the parkin in a well-buttered shallow pan in a moderate oven   Note: this cake improves by keeping a few days.

improves by keeping a few days.

LEICESTERSHIRE

MELTON MOWBRAY PORK PIES

4 lbs. of pork cut in small dice.
2 ozs. of salt, and half this quantity of black pepper.
1¼ lbs. of lard.

2¾ lbs. of flour.
¾ pint of milk and water mixed.
1 egg.

To make the paste, rub ½ lb. of lard into the flour, with a teaspoonful of salt. Take the rest of the lard and put in on to boil with the milk and water. When boiling pour half on to the flour, stirring well with a wooden spoon, add the egg after beating well, and then the rest of the boiling liquid. Knead well and let it stand for ten minutes. Use about 1½ lbs. of paste for each pie—the lids extra. Shape into pork pie shape with the hands, or use a mould, keep the paste of even thickness, then fill each pie with the pork well seasoned with the pepper and salt and a little cold water to moisten. Place some tiny pieces of butter on the top of each. Then roll out lids, moisten edges, fasten securely, and twist or crimp the edge. Make a hole in the centre, and decorate the top with leaves of pastry, brush all over with egg and bake about two hours. Keep the temperature high for the first few minutes to set the pastry in shape, and then reduce the heat.

Make some stock from the trimmings of meat and bone, until it jellies. Season with pepper and salt, skim off any fat, and strain through a funnel into the hole in the centre of the pies when they are cooling. The pies and the stock should both be lukewarm.

WHETSTONE CAKES, 1741

¼ lb. of flour.   1 teaspoonful of carraway seeds.
¼ lb. of castor sugar.   3 eggs.
             A little rose water to flavour.

Mix the flour, sugar, and carraway seeds together, then beat
up one yolk with the whites of three eggs, add the rose water
and mix to a stiff paste. Roll out as thin as a wafer, and cut
them into rounds with a wineglass. Lay them on flowered
paper and bake them in a slow oven.

MEDLEY PIE

¼ lb. of cold roast pork.   ¼ pint of good ale.
The same of cold roast beef.   Short crust pastry to cover.
1 lb. of apples, cored and sliced
   thinly.

Fill the pie dish with alternate layers of meat and apples
and season each layer with pepper, salt, and powdered ginger.
Pour the ale over the ingredients; cover with the pastry and
bake for about an hour and a half. This pie should be served
hot.

add the rosewater

LINCOLNSHIRE

LINCOLNSHIRE BRAWN

½ pig's head.   2 pig's feet.
2 hocks.   1 tablespoonful of dried sage.
                    Pepper and salt.

Put all the ingredients into a large saucepan with sufficient cold water to cover, and boil until the meat easily comes away from the bone. Remove all the bones and then cut up the meat into small pieces. Strain the stock and pour it over the meat, mixing it all well together; return to the saucepan and boil it up. It is then ready to be put into moulds, previously wetted. Do not put too much stock with the meat; the remainder can be used for broth or soup.

BOSTON APPLE PUDDING

9 apples.   2 ozs. of moist sugar.
Cinnamon, cloves.   2 eggs.
½ lemon.   ¼ lb. of butter.
                    A little grated nutmeg.

Peel, core, and slice the apples, put them in a white enamelled stewpan, with a little water, a little cinnamon, one clove, and the rind of half a lemon. Cook till quite soft, and pass through a hair sieve. Mix in the butter, sugar, yolks of the two eggs and one white, lastly the lemon juice, and beat the mixture well together. Line the inside of a pie dish with puff paste, decorate the edges, put in the apple mixture, and bake half an hour.

GRANTHAM: WHITE GINGERBREAD

1 lb. of flour.	2 eggs.
½ lb. of castor sugar.	1 dessertspoonful of baking powder.
½ lb. of butter.	
1½ ozs. of ground ginger.	

Cream the butter and sugar, then beat in the yolks of eggs one at a time, sift in the flour, baking powder, and ginger lightly, a little at a time. Lastly, whip up the whites of the eggs and fold them into the mixture. Bake on buttered greased paper in a moderate oven, and keep them quite pale in colour.

MOCK GOOSE

Leg of pork.
Sage and onion stuffing.

Parboil the leg, which must be of fresh pork, then take off the skin and remove the bone. Stuff the vacant place with sage and onion. Truss into the shape of a goose, and roast, basting it well with dripping or butter, until it is cooked through, and of a nice brown colour. Serve with apple sauce and some made gravy.

The seasoning is made with ¼ lb. of breadcrumbs, 4 onions, 10 sage leaves finely chopped, 2 ozs. of butter, and pepper and salt.

For the apple sauce, pare, core, and slice eight apples and cook them in a white enamelled saucepan, with three or four table-spoonfuls of water, until quite tender; add a little butter and brown sugar and beat them to a pulp. Serve in a sauce boat.

The gravy is made from ½ pint of stock or water, 1 carrot, 1 onion, 1 oz. of butter, ¼ oz. of flour, a little pepper and salt, a little browning.

Mince about a teaspoonful each of onion and carrot, put

the butter into a small stewpan, and when melted stir in the flour quite smoothly, and let the flour cook well in the butter; then add the minced vegetables and seasoning, and let all fry together until brown. Then add the $\frac{1}{2}$ pint of water or stock gradually, stirring well until it boils. Let it simmer for a quarter of an hour, skimming it well. Then strain it, and it is ready to serve. This gravy may be varied in flavour by adding one tomato finely minced, a mushroom or a pickled gherkin, and so on, cooking them with the carrot and onion. Add a few drops of browning.

Mock Goose

MIDDLESEX

LONDON BUNS

2 lbs. of flour.	¼ lb. of castor sugar.
1 oz. of yeast.	1 oz. of candied orange peel
1 pint of warm milk.	(cut small).
3 ozs. of butter.	

Sift the flour and sugar into a basin and test the yeast with a little of the sugar—about a large teaspoonful. Melt the butter in a saucepan, add the milk, and heat gently until lukewarm. Pour the warm milk and melted butter into the centre of the flour and mix all together with the peel into a dough. Let it rise in a warm place for about two hours. Knead and form into round buns; this quantity should make twenty-four. Place them on a greased baking sheet and let them prove. Bake in a quick oven, and directly they come from the oven brush them over with equal quantities of egg and sugar mixed, to glaze them.

GREENWICH WHITEBAIT

Whitebait is at its best in July and August; and Ministers of the Crown hold an annual whitebait dinner at the Trafalgar, Greenwich, to signalize the close of the parliamentary session.

Spread a cloth on the table, and dredge plenty of flour on it, toss the whitebait gently in the cloth, till quite dry, and then put them into the frying basket. The fat for frying must be smoking hot, at a temperature of not less than 400°. Plunge the whitebait in for one moment, that they may be crisp but not brown. Let them drain on some kitchen paper,

and serve them piled high on a dish.   Brown bread and butter
and a cut lemon should be handed with them.

DEVILLED WHITEBAIT

After the first frying, sprinkle black pepper and cayenne
over, but no more flour, and plunge them again into the fat to
brown.   Half a pint of whitebait makes a good dish.

Ministers of the Crown

NORFOLK

NORFOLK DUMPLINGS

TAKE ½ quartern of dough from that made for bread, or set a little dough made with

1 lb. of flour.	1 teaspoonful of castor sugar.
½ oz. of yeast.	¼ pint of hot water.

A little milk.

Cream the yeast and sugar together, then mingle the milk and water and pour on to the yeast. Put the flour in a basin, make a well in the centre, and pour in the milk and yeast. Mix into a dough, and allow to rise for one and a half to two hours. Then knead well, and form into dumplings. Let these stand for ten minutes. Then plunge them into boiling water, and let them boil for twenty minutes. They must be served directly they are dished, and lightly torn at the top with two forks. They are usually eaten with thick brown meat gravy, and sometimes cold with butter and sugar.

Another recipe, dated 1765:

Mix a good thick batter as for pancakes with ½ pint of milk, two eggs, a little salt, and flour. Have ready a clean saucepan of water boiling, into which drop some of this batter. Be sure that the water boils fast, and boil for two or three minutes; then throw them into a sieve to drain the water away. Then turn them into a dish and stir a lump of fresh butter into them. Eat them hot and they are very good.

NORFOLK BIFFINS, 1882

Take some Norfolk biffins, choosing the clearest rinds without
any blemishes, lay them on clean straw on baking wire, and
cover well with more straw. Set them in a very slow oven
for four or five hours. Draw them out and press them very
gently, otherwise the skins will burst. Return them to the
oven for another hour, then press them again. When cold,
rub them over with some clarified sugar. These are the dried
biffins sold in Norwich.

YARMOUTH BLOATERS

Bloaters are cured by being steeped in brine for twenty-
four hours, and then hung up and smoked. There are various
ways of cooking them. A very general way is to cut off the
head and tail, open the bloater down the back and bone it;
or it may be cooked without removing the backbone, but the
former is the nicer way. Broil the bloaters in front of (or over)
a clear fire, turning them from side to side, and serve hot.
Bloater's roes on toast are very nice as a breakfast dish, with
tiny pieces of grilled bacon; they also make an excellent after-
dinner savoury. The soft roes only should be used. Dip the
roes in oiled butter, sprinkle with cayenne, and fry gently to a
golden brown. Serve very hot on finger pieces of hot buttered
toast, and garnish with watercress.

cut off the head and tail

NORTHAMPTONSHIRE

CHEESE CAKES

2 ozs. of currants.
1 oz. of butter.
1½ ozs. of sugar.
1 egg.

1 pint of milk.
Essence of almonds.
Some grated lemon rind.
Nutmeg.

Some short or flaky pastry.

Stir the butter, sugar, and eggs in a saucepan over a gentle heat until thick, taking care not to let it boil. Boil 1 pint of sour milk (or new milk with half a dessertspoonful of vinegar or lemon juice to curdle it) until it separates into curds and whey. Strain off the curd, press well, and when cold add it to the cheesecake mixture together with the currants, spice, etc. Line some patty pans with short or flaky pastry, fill with the mixture, and bake in a brisk oven for about ten minutes.

NORTHUMBERLAND

NORTHUMBRIAN GIRDLE CAKES

½ lb. of flour.	1 teaspoonful of baking powder.
2 ozs. of currants.	¼ teaspoonful of salt.
¼ lb. of margarine or lard.	A little milk.

Mix the margarine, baking powder, and salt well into the flour, add the currants and sufficient milk to make into a soft dough. Roll out, cut into small round cakes with a cutter, and bake on a hot girdle. Split open and butter.

PICKLED SALMON

Take as much of the salmon as is required, and boil the fish in salt and water, just enough to cover it. Take it up and drain away all the liquor, and when cold put it in a deep dish and pour over equal quantities of the liquor it was boiled in, and the best vinegar and white wine, seasoned with mace, cloves, and pepper. Let it remain a day, and then serve it hot, warmed up in the pickle liquor.

PAN HAGGERTY

1 lb. of potatoes.	¼ lb. of cheese.
½ lb. of onions.	Pepper and salt.
A little dripping.	

Wash and peel the potatoes and cut in very thin slices, dry in a cloth. Peel the onions and also cut these in thin slices and shred the cheese. Then make a little dripping hot in a frying pan, spread over it first a layer of potatoes, then of onions, then cheese, and a final layer of potatoes at the top, seasoning each layer with pepper and salt. Fry gently until nearly cooked through, then either turn in the pan to brown the top or brown the haggerty before the fire.

NORTHUMBRIAN GIRDLE CAKES

¼ lb. of flour.   1 oz. of currants.
2 ozs. of lard.   ½ teaspoonful of baking powder.
Salt and a little milk.

Use just sufficient milk to make a soft dough. Roll out and cut into small rounds. Cook on a girdle.

D

NOTTINGHAMSHIRE

MANSFIELD PUDDING

2 ozs. of breadcrumbs.
½ pint of milk.
2 eggs.
1 tablespoonful of sherry or brandy.

½ oz. of castor sugar.
3 ozs. of suet, shredded finely.
3 ozs. of flour.
3 ozs. of currants.
A little grated nutmeg.

Put the suet into the flour, then mix in all the dry ingredients; beat up the eggs, mix with the brandy and milk, and beat all well together for about three minutes. Pour into a buttered pie dish and bake about one hour. Turn out on to a dish to serve, and sprinkle castor sugar over.

beat all well together

OXFORDSHIRE

OXFORD SAUSAGES

1 lb. of pork.
1 lb. of veal.
1 lb. of beef suet.
¼ lb. of breadcrumbs (slightly moistened in stock).

Half the peel of a lemon grated.
6 sage leaves, finely chopped.
Grated nutmeg.
Pepper, salt, thyme, and a little marjoram.

Pass the pork, veal, and suet through the mincing machine, mince the herbs and mix all the ingredients well together. Form them into sausage shapes, egg and breadcrumb each, and fry them.

OXFORD PUDDING, 1765

¼ lb. of biscuit grated.
¼ lb. of currants washed and picked.
¼ lb. of suet shredded finely.

½ large spoonful of powder sugar.
A very little salt, and some grated nutmeg.

Mix all well together with two yolks of eggs and make it up in balls as big as a turkey's egg. Fry them in butter until a fine light brown. You must mind to keep the pan shaking about.

For sauce, have melted butter and sugar, with a little dash of white wine.

BANBURY APPLE PIE

A layer of apples, sliced.
A layer of candied peel, chopped.

A sprinkle of currants, and
A little ground cinnamon and ginger.

Over this pour a little warm butter, and proceed with another layer. Then pour over all a cupful of boiling water, well sweetened. Cover with short crust and bake. Glaze the paste when baked, with milk and sugar, directly it comes from the oven.

For the short crust the following ingredients are required:

$\frac{1}{4}$ lb. of flour.
2 ozs. of butter.
$\frac{1}{2}$ teaspoonful of baking powder.

2 ozs. of lard.
1 oz. of castor sugar.

Rub the butter and lard lightly into the flour; then add the baking powder and castor sugar, and mix into a stiff paste with cold water. Roll this out once and it is ready for use.

BANBURY CAKES

$\frac{1}{2}$ oz. of yeast.
1 gill of warm milk.
1 lb. of flour.
$\frac{1}{4}$ lb. of currants.

$\frac{1}{4}$ lb. of mixed candied peel.
$\frac{1}{4}$ oz. of mixed ground spice.
$\frac{1}{4}$ lb. of honey.
Some puff pastry.

Banbury cakes are spoken of by Philemon Holland and Ben Jonson as far back as 1608 and 1604; but were not popular until Betty White brought them into favour about the year 1760. The Banbury firm of Betts's claim descent from the famous Betty White, and the Banbury cakes sold by them are made from the original recipe.

Let the yeast, flour, and milk work a little after forming a sponge—then add the currants, washed and picked, the candied peel finely chopped, the spice, and lastly the honey. Mix all well together, and use about a tablespoonful of this mixture for each Banbury cake, which should be made of puff paste rather less than a ¼ in. thick, and cut into rounds about 4 ins. in diameter. The mixture is then put in the centre—the two sides folded close over in the shape of an oval—turn over so that the join is underneath, press it flat with the hand, wash over with a little castor sugar and milk, cut the paste across twice in a slanting direction. Bake it a nice light colour; they will take about a quarter of an hour to bake.

Ben Jonson

SHROPSHIRE

SHREWSBURY CAKES

1 lb. of butter.	1½ lbs. of flour.
1 lb. of castor sugar.	½ gill of cream, and 1 lemon.
	1 egg.

Cream the butter and sugar well, mix in the egg, then the flour and grated lemon rind and a squeeze of lemon juice, lastly the cream. Turn out on to a pastry board and knead it well, then leave it for half an hour. Roll it out thinly, cut into small rounds, placing them on a buttered baking sheet with a flat-bladed knife. Bake about ten minutes, in a moderate oven, until they are done, and of a pale lemon colour.

SHREWSBURY CAKES, 1765

Take 2 lbs. of flour, 1 lb. of sugar finely searched, mix them together (take out ¼ lb. to roll them in); take four eggs; four spoonfuls of cream, and two spoonfuls of rose water, beat them well together and mix them with the flour into a paste; roll them into thin cakes and bake them in a quick oven.

BUCKWHEAT CAKES

1 teacupful of brewer's yeast.   Buckwheat meal.
3 pints of warm water.   A little butter.
A pinch of salt.

Mix the yeast with the warm water, and stir in as much buckwheat as will make a good batter, and sprinkle in the salt. Cover up, and let it stand in a warm place to rise. When risen and full of bubbles, butter a frying pan and pour in a ladle spoonful of the batter, and cook the same as for pancakes. Butter the cakes whilst hot, and serve them piled on a hot plate the right side up. The batter will have to stand for from two to three hours.

a pinch of salt

SHROPSHIRE PIE, 1765

To make a Shropshire pie, first make a good paste crust, then cut two rabbits to pieces, with 2 lbs. of fat pork cut into little pieces; season with pepper and salt to your liking. Then line your dish with crust and lay in your rabbits, and mix the pork with them. Take the livers of the rabbits, parboil them, and beat them in a mortar with as much fat bacon, a little sweet herbs, and some oysters if you have them; season with pepper, salt, and nutmeg; mix up with the yolk of an egg and make it into balls. Lay them here and there in your pie, some artichoke bottoms, cut in dice and cockscombs. Grate a little nutmeg over the meat, then put in ½ pint of red wine and ½ pint of water. Close your pie and bake it an hour and a half in a quick oven, but not too fierce an oven.

SOMERSETSHIRE

BATH BUNS

1 lb. of Vienna flour.
½ oz. of German yeast.
1 teaspoonful of castor sugar.
1 gill of tepid milk.
2 ozs. of sultanas.

4 ozs. of butter.
2 ozs. of castor sugar.
3 ozs. of candied peel.
3 eggs.
2 ozs. of crushed lump sugar.

A few carraway comfits.

Cream the yeast with the teaspoonful of castor sugar, add the tepid milk, and strain into half the flour to form a sponge. Let it rise for an hour, then rub the butter into the other ½ lb. of flour, adding sultanas, castor sugar, and candied peel, and the sponge from the other basin. Now, with the hand, beat in the eggs well, one at a time, and set it to rise again. When well risen, form into twelve rocky buns, sprinkle the crushed lump sugar on top, also a few carraway comfits. Let them prove, then bake from ten to fifteen minutes.

BATH SALLY LUNNS

Sally Lunns derive their name from the original maker and inventor, Miss Sally Lunn, who was born and lived in Bath, and sent out this dainty in various sizes, toasted hot and buttered, to all the large tea parties of a hundred years ago. The ingredients are:

2 lbs. of fine flour, sifted.
2 ozs. of castor sugar.
¼ lb. of butter.

4 eggs.
1 pint of milk.
¼ pint of brewer's yeast.

Put 1½ lbs. of the flour in a basin and mix with the yeast and ¼ pint of warm milk. Cover it over and let it stand in a

sent out this dainty in various sizes

warm place until it has risen as high as it will (one can generally allow it about two hours). Into the remaining $\frac{1}{4}$ lb. of flour rub the butter and mix in the sugar. Add this to the sponge in the basin, then well beat in the eggs—one at a time. Allow to stand for half an hour, then knead the mixture and put a portion into Sally Lunn tins, filling them about half full. Let them stand until the dough has risen to the top of the tin, then bake them in a quick oven. To glaze the top, brush over with equal quantities of castor sugar and milk immediately they are taken from the oven. The Sally Lunns are cut in slices, well toasted and well buttered, and served whole.

AN OLD RECIPE FOR CHEDDAR CHEESE (1741)

Take the new milk of six cows in the morning, and the evening cream of six others, and put three spoonfuls of rennet to it. When it is come, break it and whey it. Then do this again, work into the curd $1\frac{1}{2}$ lbs. of fresh butter, and put it in your press and turn it very often for an hour or more. Put wet cloths at first to the cheese, but, towards the last, two or three fine dry cloths. Let the cheese lie thirty hours in the press, then take it out, wash it in whey, and lay in a dry cloth. When dry, lay it on a shelf and turn it often.

BATH OLIVER BISCUITS

The Bath Oliver biscuits, well known all the world over, were invented about one hundred and fifty years ago by Dr. Oliver, a famous physician. They were primarily intended for the use of his patients. There is no sugar in the preparation, which makes them a good food for dyspeptics. The secret has been well kept, but one can ensure having the genuine article by observing that the biscuit is stamped with a portrait of the inventor, and they are put up in curious tall tins to fit the size of the biscuit. In an old cookery book, dated 1831, I found this recipe for Oliver's biscuits, which may be similar: One

for the use of his patients

large spoonful of yeast in two spoonfuls of new milk and 1½ lbs. of flour. Let it rise half an hour. Melt 2 ozs. of butter, add ¼ oz. of white sugar and enough warm milk to make the flour into a dough. Roll out thin, cut into biscuits, prick well, and bake in a middling hot oven.

SOMERSET FRUMENTY

1 pint of wheat.	2 eggs.
1 pint of water.	Sugar to sweeten.
1 pint of milk.	A little nutmeg.
1 tablespoonful of dried currants.	

Bruise the wheat with a pestle and mortar, put it in a stone jar, pour the water on it, and bake in a slow oven for about three hours, until the wheat is soft. Then add the milk, sugar and flavouring, and currants. Stir the mixture until the currants are soft. Now add the beaten yolks of the eggs and stir over the fire for a few minutes, taking care to see that the frumenty does not boil. Serve in a deep dish.

BATH CHAPS

Bath chap was a very favourite dish in the early part of the nineteenth century, and at that time was unobtainable elsewhere. It is the lower half of a small pig's head divided and cured with sugar and spices, and dried or smoked in the same manner as hams. For cooking, the Bath chap should be soaked for a few hours in cold water and then cooked gently for about two hours. The skin should be removed when taken up, and the Bath chap covered with raspings and served as a cold breakfast dish.

BATH POLONIES

Bath polony is somewhat similar to a German sausage, but is very much smaller—about 2½ ins. long—and of about the same circumference. It is much more delicate, and has a tiny layer of fat next to the scarlet skin.

Bath Chaps

STAFFORDSHIRE

LEMON SYLLABUBS, 1741

1 pint of cream.   Juice of 2 lemons, the rind of
¼ lb. of sugar.   one grated.
½ pint of white wine.

Mix all these together and mix it up as fast as you can, till it is thick. Then pour the mixture into glasses and let it stand for five or six hours; it can be made overnight.

WHIP SYLLABUB, 1822

¼ lb. of sugar.   ½ gill of brandy.
The juice and grated rind of   ½ gill of sweet wine.
    1 lemon.   1½ pints of good cream.

Whisk the whole well, take off the froth as it rises with a skimmer and put it on a sieve, continue to whisk until you have enough. Then nearly fill the custard glasses with the mixture, and lay on some of the whipped froth with a spoon.

SUFFOLK

IPSWICH ALMOND PUDDING

The following is an old recipe (1741):

1½ ozs. of breadcrumbs.	A little rose or orange flower
¾ pt. of cream.	water.
¼ lb. of ground almonds.	4 eggs.
2 ozs. of castor sugar.	

Make the cream hot and pour it on the crumbs, then stir in the sugar, almonds, and flavouring. Beat up four yolks and two whites of eggs, mix well with the other ingredients, and pour into a buttered pie dish, putting a few little pieces of butter at the top. Let it bake for half an hour in a slow oven.

SUFFOLK BUNS

1 lb. of flour or ground rice.	2 eggs.
¼ lb. of lard or butter.	2 teaspoonfuls of baking
3 ozs. of sugar.	powder.
3 ozs. of currants or 1½ ozs. of	A pinch of salt.
carraway seeds.	A very little milk.

Rub the butter into the flour, then add all the dry ingredients. Beat up the eggs, add them, and make a smooth, firm paste, using as little milk as possible. Roll out 1 in. thick, cut into rounds, and bake on a buttered baking sheet in a moderate oven.

cut into small rounds

ALDEBURGH SPRATS

Sprats may be smoked, dried, potted, or fried; but being very oily, they are best broiled. They are in season in November and during the winter.

To broil sprats, clean them well, dry them and roll or toss lightly in flour. Broil on a closely barred gridiron over a clear fire or under the gas griller. Turn them in about three minutes.

If preferred, they may be cooked in a hot dry frying pan, as there is sufficient oil in the fish to prevent them sticking or burning. As with whitebait, their flavour is improved by the addition of a little lemon juice and cayenne pepper.

BROILED PARTRIDGE

Take two or three partridges, split in halves. Sprinkle lightly with flour, salt, and cayenne pepper, and broil them over a clear fire, the cut side first. Brush over with some hot butter when dished, and serve with the following sauce:

KETCHUP SAUCE

2 ozs. of butter.
1 oz. of flour.
½ pint of brown stock.

2 large tablespoonfuls of mushroom ketchup.
Salt and cayenne.

Melt the butter in a stewpan, stir in the flour, cayenne, and salt, and cook for two minutes. Then gradually add the stock, let it boil up well, add the ketchup, and strain into a sauce boat.

SUFFOLK RUSKS

1 lb. of flour.	3 eggs.
1 tablespoonful of brewer's yeast.	2 ozs. of castor sugar.
	¼ pint. of milk.

2 ozs. of butter.

Melt the butter in the milk. Mix the flour and sugar in a basin, add the yeast and warm butter and milk, then beat in the eggs and form a smooth dough. Let this stand to rise for one and a half hours, then knead and divide into sixteen pieces. Roll these about 3 ins. long and bake for ten minutes. Take them from the oven, pull them in half lengthwise, and put them back in the oven to get crisp. These are the sweet rusks. If wanted in place of bread or biscuits, omit the sugar.

pull them in half

SURREY

RICHMOND MAIDS OF HONOUR

These delicious little cheese cakes are said to derive their name from the maids of honour of Queen Elizabeth, who had a palace at Richmond. The recipe given below is taken from a cookery manuscript in Queen Elizabeth's time.

Sift ¼ lb. of dry curd, mix it well with 6 ozs. of good butter, break the yolks of four eggs into another basin, and a glass of brandy; add to it 6 ozs. of powdered lump sugar, and beat well together one very floury baked potato cold, 1 oz. of sweet almonds and the same quantity of bitter almonds pounded, the grated rind of three lemons, the juice of one, and half a nutmeg grated. Mix these well together and add to the curds and butter; stir well up. Line some tartlet tins with good paste, and place some of the above mixture in, and bake quickly.

The original " Maid of Honour " shop in Hill Street, Richmond, continues to supply this dainty little cheese cake. The following recipe is very good:

Line some patty pans with good puff paste and fill with a mixture made with the ingredients given below:

½ pint of milk.	2 ozs. of ground almonds.
2 tablespoonfuls of bread-crumbs.	1 oz. of sugar.
	The grated rind of one lemon.
4 ozs. of butter.	3 eggs.

Boil the milk and crumbs and let it stand for ten minutes, then add the butter, sugar, and flavouring; beat in the three eggs, one at a time. Put a dessertspoonful of this into the centre of the lined patty pans, and bake a golden brown.

SUSSEX

LARDY JOHNS

½ lb. of flour.
¼ lb. of lard.
1½ teaspoonfuls of baking powder.

1 oz. of sugar.
½ oz. of currants.
¼ pint of water.

Rub the lard into the flour, then add the baking powder mixed with the sugar; last of all put in the currants after they have been thoroughly picked over and cleaned. Mix into a stiff paste with the water; roll out, cut into 2-in. squares, and bake for about ten to fifteen minutes.

SUSSEX HEAVIES

2 breakfastcupfuls of flour.
2 ozs. of lard.
1 oz. of castor sugar.

2 oz. currants or sultanas.
1 teacupful of milk soured by adding juice of half a lemon.

Rub lard into flour, then add the sugar and currants, lastly soured milk to make the mixture the consistency of pastry. Roll out as for pastry, and cut into small rounds. Bake for fifteen minutes in a moderate oven, after brushing over with the remains of soured milk.

E

Sussex Heavies

SUSSEX PUDDING

1 lb. of strawberries.	¼ lb. of castor sugar.
½ pint of water.	

Cook until soft and rub through a hair sieve.

Put 1 pint of milk, ½ oz. French gelatine, 1½ ozs. of sugar, into a saucepan, and just let it boil. Stir until the gelatine is dissolved and strain into a jug. Put the fruit pulp into a glass dish, and pour the milk over carefully just before it sets. Serve very cold.

SUSSEX FRITTERS

½ lb. of cold boiled potatoes.	1 egg.
2 ozs. of finely minced ham.	Pepper and salt.
A teaspoonful of chopped parsley.	

Put the potatoes through a potato masher, then mix in the minced ham, parsley, and seasoning, with the beaten yolk of the egg. Shape into small balls, egg and breadcrumb them, and fry a golden brown.

SUSSEX PUDDING
(*To eat with meat*)

1 lb. of flour.	6 ozs. of suet.
A little baking powder.	

Shred the suet finely and chop it lightly. Mix with the flour and baking powder and use about ½ pint of cold water to mix the pudding. Knead and shape into a roly-poly, scald and flour a cloth, tie up the pudding, and plunge it into boiling water, letting it boil quickly for an hour. Take it up and cut it into slices ½ in. thick. Lay these in the dripping pan under the meat which is roasting, so that they may get saturated with the dripping, and nicely brown on the top. Serve with the roast meat in the same manner as a Yorkshire pudding. Sometimes this pudding is served as a separate course just before the meat.

WESTMORLAND

DERWENTWATER CAKES

1 lb. flour.	¼ lb. of currants.
½ lb. of butter.	½ lb. of castor sugar.

4 eggs.

Separate the eggs and beat the yolks only into the butter with the sugar. Then lightly add the flour, mixing well. Lastly beat up the whites of the eggs to a very stiff froth and fold them into the cake mixture. Roll out about 1 in. thick, place on a baking tin and bake for fifteen minutes in a slow oven.

GRASMERE GINGERBREAD

8 ozs. of flour.	2 teaspoonfuls of syrup.
3 ozs. of sugar.	¼ teaspoonful of baking powder.
¼ oz. of ground ginger.	
2 yolks of eggs.	5 ozs. of butter.
2 ozs. of chopped almonds.	Lemon rind.

Vanilla.

Mix the flour, ginger, sugar, almonds, lemon rind, baking powder, and vanilla with warm butter, egg yolks, and syrup. Roll out half of the mixture, brush with egg and milk, sprinkle with chopped peel or chopped preserved ginger. Roll remainder of the mixture and put over the peel, and brush the top with egg or milk. Sprinkle on almonds and sugar. Put on greased baking sheet, bake slowly for thirty minutes.

THREE DECKERS

1 lb. of short crust.　　　　　Any kind of cooking fruit.
Moist sugar.

Line a Yorkshire pudding tin with short crust (see p. 68) about ⅛ in. thick, then put a layer of fruit, cut up the same as for a tart; if it should happen to be either apples or rhubarb, sprinkle moist sugar over. Then cover with a layer of short crust, and repeat the process until there are three layers of fruit. Cover lastly with the pastry and bake about one hour. For a raspberry and currant three decker, the centre layer could be raspberries, and for blackberry and apple the centre layer might consist of apples.

at Grasmere

WILTSHIRE

DEVIZES PIE

Some slices of cold calf's head. Slices of bacon.
A few slices of cold lamb. Three hard-boiled eggs.
Some of the calf's brains and Spice, cayenne pepper, and
tongue. salt.

Pastry to cover.

Season all the slices of meat well and arrange them in layers
in a pie dish with the eggs cut into rings, then fill up the dish
with a rich clear gravy; or use some of the liquor the calf's
head was boiled in, reducing it first to a good jelly. Cover
the pie with a good crust and bake it in a slow oven. Turn it
out when cold on to a dish; the paste must be underneath;
garnish around the edge with sprigs of parsley and send to
table.

a good crust

WORCESTERSHIRE

WORCESTER SAUCE

1 pint of brown vinegar.

3 tablespoonfuls of walnut ketchup.

2 tablespoonfuls of essence anchovy.

2 tablespoonfuls of soy.

$\frac{1}{4}$ teaspoonful of cayenne.

2 finely chopped shallots.

A little salt.

Mix the ingredients and cork closely in a large bottle, shake it two or three times a day for a fortnight. Strain and bottle for use.

shake it two or three
times a day —

YORKSHIRE

YORKSHIRE CHRISTMAS PIE
(An old recipe, 1765*)*

FIRST make a good standing crust, let the wall and bottom be very thick; bone by opening down the back, a turkey, a goose, a fowl, a partridge, and a pigeon. Season them all very well, using ½ oz. of mace, nutmeg, and black pepper, ¼ oz. of cloves, two large spoonfuls of salt, and mix them together. First bone the pigeon, then the partridge, cover them one with the other; then the fowl, the goose, and the turkey, which must be large, covering each bird in turn, so that at the last it looks like one large turkey. Lay the turkey in the pie and fill up the corners with hare or woodcock cut in small pieces. Fill the pie closely and put at least 4 lbs. of fresh butter on the top. Cover with a thick lid of paste and let the pie be well baked for at least four hours. This crust will take a bushel of flour.

These pies are often sent to London in a box as presents, therefore the walls must be well built.

A Standing Crust for Great Pies.

Take a peck of flour, and 6 lbs. of butter boiled in a gallon of water ; skim it off into the flour and as little of the liquor as you can. Work it well up into a paste, then pull it into pieces until it is cold, and then make it up what form you will have it. This is fit for the walls of a Turkey Pye

TO CURE A YORK HAM

Take—

1 lb. of common salt.	1¼ ozs. of saltpetre.
½ lb. of bay salt.	½ oz. of moist sugar.

Sprinkle some salt over the leg of pork, and leave to drain for a few hours. Then mix the above ingredients together, and rub well into every part of the leg. Put into a deep pan and leave for three of four days, turning it every day. Now pour over it 1 lb. of treacle, and let it remain in pickle for three weeks, turning it as is usual every day. After that time put it to soak in cold water for twenty-four hours, and either boil or bake it.

To Boil a Ham.—Dry the ham, scrape it, and pare away any discoloured spots. Lay it in a large saucepan, cover it with lukewarm water, and add to this just a little vinegar. Bring it slowly to the boil, carefully skim, then put in a bunch of sweet herbs and two or three carrots. Simmer very slowly, allowing half an hour to the pound. When sufficiently cooked, take it up, strip off the skin, and cover it at once with raspings. It should remain uncut till cold.

To Bake a Ham.—Soak the ham for twenty-four hours, then lay it in a deep pan, and place an oiled paper on the top. Cover with a crust made of flour and water, and bake in a moderate oven for some hours, allowing about half an hour to each pound. When baked, remove the crust, the oiled paper, and the rind. Either cover with raspings whilst hot, or leave until cold and glaze it. A small piece of gammon is very good cooked this way.

NORTH COUNTRY SWEET PIE

2 ozs. of fat mutton chops.	2 ozs. of candied peel.
2 ozs. of currants, raisins, and sultanas.	The juice of 1 lemon.
6 ozs. of moist sugar.	A little grated cinnamon, mace, nutmeg.
2 wineglasses of rum.	Pepper and salt to taste.

Puff pastry.

Cut the mutton into ½-in. squares. Put alternate layers in a piedish of meat and fruit and season each layer. Pour the rum over, cover with puff pastry, and bake. This is a favourite Christmas dish.

YORKSHIRE YULE OR SPICE CAKE

These cakes are quite an institution in Yorkshire at Christmas-time, when they are presented to friends, and also freely offered to visitors. These cakes are often eaten with cheese instead of bread, and wine or beer is handed round in glasses. To make a large quantity, use:

4 lbs. of flour.	3 lbs. of currants.
½ oz. of salt.	1½ lbs. of moist sugar.
¾ lb. of butter.	4 eggs.
1 lb. of lard.	A little grated nutmeg.

¾ pint of fresh brewer's yeast.

Rub the flour and salt through a sieve, then rub in the butter and lard. Next, make a well in the centre, pour in the yeast mixed with a pint of lukewarm water, and set to rise in the same way as for bread. Be careful to see that the yeast is not bitter. When well risen, knead, then work in the spice and currants and sugar; and lastly the eggs, which should be well beaten and added gradually. Mix thoroughly, divide into portions, fill the cake tins about half full, let them prove, and bake in a sharp oven.

freely offered to visitors

SAVOURY PUDDING

This is served with goose or duck, and sometimes with roast pork. The ingredients are—

Bread.	3 ozs. of flour.
1 tablespoonful of sage.	1 egg.
3 onions.	½ pint of milk.

Pepper and salt.

Break up half a loaf of bread into a basin with one table-spoonful of sage, finely chopped. Cut up and boil three large onions, and drain them. Chop them small and mix with three tablespoonfuls of flour, and add a little pepper and salt and one egg mixed with ½ pint of milk. The mixture should be rather stiff. Put into a pudding tin and make level with a spoon (there should be a little hot dripping in the tin before the mixture is put in). Bake for half an hour in a quick oven.

In houses where the meat is roasted before the fire, the pudding is put for a short time under the meat to catch the drippings. This also applies to Yorkshire pudding.

YORKSHIRE PARKIN

This is made in Yorkshire at all times of the year, but especially for November 5, at which time it is supposed to be eaten with mugs of hot milk, whilst standing around the bonfire.

2 lbs. of fine oatmeal.	5 lbs. of treacle.
2 lbs. of medium oatmeal.	1 oz. of ground ginger.
2 lbs. of flour.	4 eggs.
¾ lb. of butter.	6 small teaspoonfuls of bicar-
¾ lb. of lard.	bonate of soda.

Rub the lard and butter into the flour and oatmeal, warm the treacle, and pour into the dry ingredients. Dissolve the bicarbonate of soda in a glass of beer, and mix all well together,

especially on November 5 th

making the dough so that it will drop (not run) off the spoon.
Bake in well-buttered tins.

Do not have the oven too hot, as the parkin soon burns,
and be careful not to fill the tins too full.

YORKSHIRE FIRMETY

This is Yorkshire porridge made by slightly crushing ½ lb.
of wheat berries with a pestle and mortar. Then put the
wheat in a covered jar with 1½ pints of skim milk. Let it
cook very gently for twelve hours in a slow oven, take it out
and stir it now and then, and add a little more milk if necessary.
This will keep good for some days, and may be served hot or
cold. To serve it, take two or three tablespoonfuls of the
" cree," mix it with about ½ pint of new milk, a little sugar,
1 oz. of stoned raisins, and a pinch of spice, and send to table
either hot or cold, as preferred. (Firmety is pronounced
frummety.)

YORKSHIRE BARLEY PORRIDGE

This is made in the same way as the above, using pearl barley
instead of coarse oatmeal, and a little grated nutmeg instead of
the spice.

WEST RIDING PUDDING

Take the weight of 2 eggs in flour and sugar, a few drops
of vanilla essence, 2 tablespoonfuls of jam, and 1 teaspoonful of
baking powder.

Butter a small pie dish and put in the layer of jam. Whip
the eggs and sugar for five minutes, and, lastly, stir in the
flour, baking powder, and flavouring. Put this mixture on the
top of the jam, and bake for about half an hour.

YORK BISCUIT

2 lbs. of flour.	1 dessertspoonful of baking
¾ lb. of butter.	powder.
¾ lb. castor sugar.	½ pint of milk.

Cream the butter and the sugar together, mix the baking powder with the flour, then, gradually, add first the milk and then the flour, until the whole is worked into a smooth dough. Let it stand for an hour. Then roll it out as thin as a penny, and stamp out with a round biscuit stamp cutter. Bake in a moderate oven.

YORKSHIRE PUDDING

¼ lb. of flour.	¼ pint of milk.
2 eggs.	¼ pint of water.
	Pinch of salt.

Pass the flour through a sieve into a basin, and add a pinch of salt. Make a well in the centre and break the eggs into it. Add a little of the milk, and mix gradually and smoothly, then more and more, until all the milk is in. Beat well for ten minutes, and then mix in the water. Let the batter stand for at least half an hour before using, so that the mixtures may get cold. Pour into a well-greased tin and bake under the meat.

An Old Recipe for Yorkshire Pudding (1765)

Take a quart of milk, four eggs, and a little salt, and make it up into a thick batter with flour, like a pancake batter. You must have a good piece of meat at the fire. Take a stewpan and put some dripping in, set it on the fire, and when it boils pour in your pudding. Let it bake on the fire until you think it is high enough, then turn a plate upside down in the dripping pan, that the pan may not be blacked, set your stewpan on it under your meat and let the dripping drop on the pudding, and the heat of the fire come to it, to make it a fine brown. When your meat is done and sent to table, drain all the fat from your pudding and set it on the fire to dry a little; then slide it as dry as you can into a dish, melt some butter, and pour it into a cup and set it in the middle of the pudding. It is an excellent good pudding, and the gravy of the meat eats well with it.

OVEN CAKE

When bread is being made and the dough is ready to bake, take half of the dough and form it into a ball, then roll this out into a round measuring about 12 ins. across. Place it on a baking sheet and prick it well with a fork, right through to the tin. Let it prove, then bake it in a hot oven until firm. Split it in halves, butter it well, and serve at once.

YORKSHIRE TEA CAKES

These are made with the following ingredients:

1½ lbs. of flour.	3 oz. of butter.
¾ pint of milk.	2 eggs.
¼ pint of brewer's yeast.	

Make a sponge with the flour, the yeast and the milk (which must be warm, and the butter dissolved in it). Let it rise well, work in the eggs, then turn out and knead. Make up into small rounds about the size of a tea saucer. Flatten them with the hand and put them to prove on a flat greased baking tin. When well risen, bake them in a sharp oven.

CHRISTMAS PLUM CAKES

7 lbs. of flour.	2 lbs. of currants.
2½ lbs. of butter.	1½ lbs. of sultanas.
4 lbs. of sugar (moist).	½ lb. of candied peel (mixed)
8 eggs.	6½ ozs. of baking powder.
About 1 quart of milk.	

flatten them with the hand

Rub the butter into the flour. Mix the baking powder and sugar together, and mingle in. Then add the fruit (washed and cleaned) and the candied peel (finely shredded). Beat up the eggs with some of the milk, then thoroughly mix with the other ingredients, gradually using all the milk. About half fill some large cake tins—which must be prepared with butter brushed over, and lightly dusted with flour—and bake the cakes in a moderate oven. They are the better for keeping, so should be made early in December.

DRIED SALMON

Some dried salmon.	1 oz. of butter.
3 hard-boiled eggs.	¼ oz. of flour.
½ pint of cream.	Pepper and salt to season.

Some mashed potatoes.

Pull the dried salmon into flakes. Cut the eggs in rather large pieces. Make a sauce with the butter, flour, cream, and seasoning. Stir in the eggs and fish, and serve with a deep border of hot mashed potato.

BUTTERED GROUSE

1 brace of grouse.	1 blade or two of mace.
¼ lb. of butter.	Pepper, salt, and cayenne.

Roast the grouse in the usual way and then cut them up into neat joints and arrange them in a pie dish. Add the butter to the hot dripping used for basting, season with the mace, cayenne pepper, and salt, and pour this over the grouse. Let it get quite cold and serve in the dish. A casserole may be used instead of a pie dish, and would look nicer on the table.

cut them into neat joints

NATIONAL

ROAST BEEF

A BARON OF BEEF weighs from forty to eighty pounds and is always roasted. The prime pieces of beef for roasting are the sirloin, or the fore rib, and before cooking it is always advisable to hang beef for a few days.

To roast beef before the fire, it is necessary first of all to make up a very good fire, and when the fire is ready, hang the joint on the roasting jack, wind it up and set it going with the beef quite close to the fire for the first ten minutes, in order to seal up the outside, forming a case to keep the red juices of the meat from escaping; then draw it back a little and cook steadily, basting the joint frequently. Allow fifteen minutes to the pound in the usual way; but if the joint is a very large one, twenty minutes would be better. For the gravy, pour nearly all the dripping away from the pan, then sprinkle in a little salt and a dust of flour and stir round with an iron spoon; then pour into it about ¾ pint of boiling water or, better still, boiling stock. Stir well and pour some round the joint when dished, and pour the remainder into a gravy boat.

Beef should be served with Yorkshire pudding (see page 68) and horse-radish sauce.

BOAR'S HEAD

Under the Norman Kings the wild boar's head was considered a noble dish, and was brought to the King's table with the trumpeters sounding their trumpets before it in pro-

brought to the King's table

cession. This custom was usual amongst the Barons and Knights in olden time. In the reign of Charles I. it was the first dish placed on the board on Christmas Day, carried into the banqueting hall on a golden dish and heralded with a jubilant flourish of trumpets. This custom still obtains at Queen's College, Oxford, where with much ceremony the boar's head is carried on a silver salver in procession.

Recipe

1 boar's head.	Some brown sugar.
1½ lbs. of salt.	1 tablespoonful of saltpetre.
	Some aromatic spices.

Remove the bones from the head and rub it with the above ingredients inside and out every day for a week (mixing the ingredients first and taking a sixth part daily). Then remove the ears, as these must be cooked separately. Stuff the head with a forcemeat composed of very finely minced pork and veal, truffles, champignons, ¼ lb. of breadcrumbs, and bind together with two eggs, season with spice, pepper, salt. A very large head may have a bullock's tongue in the centre with the stuffing round. Tie into shape with a cloth, putting a flat plate at the back of the head, and boil gently in stock for five or six hours. Take up and press the head into shape, and let it get quite cold. Cook the ears for an hour only and put them in place when cold, and make sockets for the glass eyes. Give two or three coats of glaze, put in the eyes and decorate with some butter through a forcer. The following cold sauce may be served with it: Mix together the juice and grated rind of an orange, add a little sugar and two wineglasses of port, a teaspoonful of made mustard, pepper and salt, then warm four tablespoonfuls of currant jelly and whisk everything together.

stuff the goose —

but not too full

MICHAELMAS GOOSE

The custom of eating goose at Michaelmas seems to have arisen from the practice among the rural tenantry of bringing a good stubble goose to propitiate the landlord when paying their rent. As the old rhyme has it:

> "And when the tenants come to pay their quarter's rent
> They bring some fowls at Midsummer,
> A dishe of fishe in Lent;
> At Christmas a capon, at Michaelmas a goose,
> And somewhat else at New Year's tide
> For feare their lease flie loose."
>   GEORGE GASCOIGNE.

An Old English Recipe for Roast Goose, 1741

The goose should be well picked, cleaned, and singed. Make the stuffing with 2 ozs. of onion, half as much green sage, chop them very fine, add 4 ozs. of breadcrumbs, pepper and salt to taste, and to this some cooks add half the liver, parboiling it first. Mix with the yolk and white of an egg, incorporating the whole together well. Stuff the goose but not too full, and truss into shape for roasting on the spit. An hour and a half to two hours will roast a fine goose in front of the fire. Send up apple sauce and gravy with it.

This recipe holds good in the present day, although the good old custom of roasting on the spit is no longer in vogue in private houses, but there are a few exceptions, notably in the Colleges of Oxford and Cambridge and in the mansions of some of the nobility.

MINCE PIES

Mince pies in olden times were always made in cradle-shaped tins having flat ends and a little raised. These fell into disfavour in Puritanical times and were deemed Popish and idolatrous, because the coffin or crust was supposed to represent the cradle or manger in which the Holy Child was laid; and the

F

in Puritanical times

savoury ingredients to represent the various gifts of spices brought by the three Kings. All sorts of ingredients were used in the old-fashioned mince pies. In 1596 they were called mutton pies, when they were made of a mixture of finely minced mutton. Later neat's tongue was substituted, or lean beef with a mixture of suet, fruit, candied peel, with wine, brandy, or orange flower water to moisten.

MINCEMEAT, 1741

1 lb. of cold roast beef or veal. A little salt and mixed spice.
2 lbs. of beef suet. ½ lb. of sugar.
2 pippins. 1 grated lemon rind and juice.
1 lb. of raisins of the sun. 1 lb. of currants.
¼ oz. of grated nutmeg. ½ lb. of mixed peel.

Chop the meat, suet, apples and peel finely; shred the raisins after stoning them, and then put all the ingredients together and mix them thoroughly. When making the mince pies put a little sack and claret into each.

MINCEMEAT, 1822

1 lb. of beef suet. ½ nutmeg grated.
1 lb. of apples. ¼ oz. of salt.
1½ lbs. of currants. ¼ oz. of ground ginger.
½ lb. of raisins. ½ oz. of mixed spice.
½ lb. of moist sugar. 3 lemons, the juice and rind
¾ lb. of mixed candied peel.   grated.
1 lb. of cold roast beef. ¼ pint of brandy.
¼ pint of sweet wine.

MINCE PIES

Take some patty pans and line with puff paste the thickness of a penny, then fill with mincemeat and cover with pastry a ¼ in. thick; trim the edges and bake in a quick oven. Send them to table hot and dust some castor sugar over them.

PLUM PUDDING, 1882

1½ lbs. of sugar.	6 eggs.
1½ lbs. of Malaga raisins (stoned).	Half a nutmeg grated. A little mixed spice.
2 lbs. of currants (washed and picked).	1 teaspoonful of salt. 1 lb. of suet (chopped).
¾ lb. of breadcrumbs.	6 ozs. of candied peel.
¾ lb. of flour.	1 pint of milk.

Mix all the dry ingredients together in a large pan first, then beat up the eggs and add the milk to them. Gradually mix this in with the ingredients and beat well. Put the pudding mixture into well-greased basins, tie over with a cloth and boil for five hours or steam for six.

Puddings are best when mixed an hour or so before they are boiled, to allow the various ingredients to amalgamate by that means, and the whole becomes richer and fuller of flavour, especially if the various ingredients are thoroughly stirred together.

the pudding

ROAST TURKEY

The turkey is a native of North America, and was introduced into this country during the reign of Henry VIII., and has ever since formed the chief dish on Christmas Day. Care must be always taken that the turkey is brought out of the cold larder in frosty weather and placed in the kitchen overnight, for Jack Frost has ruined the reputation of many a roaster of turkey by the bird being put to roast when it is thoroughly frozen.

To prepare the turkey make some stuffing, and stuff it under the breast where the craw was taken out, and make some of the stuffing into balls. Boil or fry these and use them to garnish the dish. A very large turkey roasted in front of a fire will take three hours and should be constantly basted; one weighing say 10 lbs. would take about two hours.

Fried pork sausages are a very usual accompaniment; and a turkey garnished with these all round the bird is called " An Alderman in Chains."

THE STUFFING FOR THE TURKEY, 1882

4 ozs. of beef marrow or suet.	1 dessertspoonful of parsley.
4 ozs. of breadcrumbs.	1 eschallot.
1 heaped teaspoonful of lemon thyme.	1½ lbs. of sausage meat.
	2 eggs.
1 heaped teaspoonful of grated lemon peel.	A little grated nutmeg, pepper and salt.

Mince the suet finely; chop up the eschallot, parsley, and lemon thyme, and mix all together with the eggs; pound it thoroughly, and use the larger portion for the stuffing for the turkey and the remainder for forcemeat balls.

GRAVY FOR TURKEY

2 ozs. of butter.	1 pint of stock.
1 oz. of flour.	Some basil, or tarragon.
½ oz. of minced onion.	Juice of half a lemon.
1 tablespoonful of mushroom catsup.	Cayenne pepper and salt to season.
1 tablespoonful of port.	

Put the butter into a stewpan and let it melt, and when quite hot cook the onion in it until it takes on a light brown colour; now sprinkle in the flour, herbs and seasoning, add the stock gradually, stirring all the time; when it boils add the port and mushroom catsup. Simmer gently for five minutes longer and then strain, and serve hot in a gravy boat.

BREAD SAUCE

1 teacupful of breadcrumbs.	12 allspice berries.
2 tablespoonfuls of cream.	1 blade of mace.
A medium-sized onion.	Cayenne pepper and salt.
¾ pint of milk.	

Boil the onion in the milk and then pour it on to the bread-crumbs and seasoning. Let it stand for an hour well covered up, after which take out the onion, mace, and allspice, add the cream and let it come gently to the boil, and serve.

TWELFTH CAKE

The celebration of Twelfth Day has much declined in England during the last half-century, but the custom is not quite obsolete; for at Drury Lane Theatre the cake is still eaten on Twelfth Night, January 6th—that is, twelve days after Christmas.

Robert Baddely, who started life as a cook, and later went on the stage (scoring a considerable success as an actor), left a legacy of £100 in order that a cake might be bought every year and eaten on Twelfth Night, and some port wine negus drunk to his memory in the green room of Drury Lane Theatre.

The Twelfth cake was a large rich cake tastefully decorated with icing and crystallised fruits. A bean was always inserted, and whoever got the piece of cake with the bean was called " King of the Bean." Hence arose the term " the lucky bean," as it was supposed to bring good luck.

Recipe

½ lb. of flour.	1 lb. of currants.
½ lb. of castor sugar	2 ozs. of blanched almonds.
½ lb. of butter.	3 ozs. of mixed candied peel.
4 eggs.	A little grated nutmeg.
½ gill of brandy.	

started life as a cook

Cream the butter, sugar and nutmeg together, beat in the eggs separately for two minutes, next stir in the brandy, and then lightly sift in the flour by degrees, add the washed currants, shredded peel and almonds. Put into a large cake tin lined with buttered paper, and bake slowly about three hours. When cold decorate with royal icing.

BRIDE OR WEDDING CAKE

Flour, butter, currants and candied peel, of each 3 lbs.	The rind of 4 oranges (grated).
2 lbs. of glacé cherries.	The rind of 4 lemons (grated).
1 lb. of ground almonds.	1 oz. of mixed spice.
16 eggs.	2 teaspoonfuls of salt.
	¼ pint of brandy.

¼ pint of rum.

Beat the butter and sugar to a cream. The flour should be sieved and dried. Cut the cherries into four, and very thinly shred the candied peel and chop. Grate the rinds of the oranges and lemons. Mix the spices and salt with the flour. When the sugar and butter is smooth and creamy, sift in some flour and some of the fruit and ground almonds; then beat in one egg and then another. Repeat the process until all the eggs and all the ingredients are in, then add the brandy. The cake mixture will take about half an hour to mix, as it requires to be thoroughly well beaten. Line two cake tins with buttered paper in double sheets; and choose one tin smaller than the other in order to have a double tier cake. If only one cake is required, use just half the above quantity. Bake in a very slow oven from five to six hours. Let a week elapse before making the almond icing.

ROYAL ICING FOR CAKES

1 lb. of icing sugar
Juice of 1 lemon.
Whites of 2 eggs.

Royal icing

Sift the icing sugar through a fine hair sieve, place the whites of the eggs in a separate basin with the strained lemon juice. Add a little of this to the icing sugar, working and beating well with a wooden spoon, then a little more, until the whole is mixed and is smooth and creamy. Spread a very thin layer over the cake, dipping the knife in cold water; let this dry and it will keep the cake crumbs in place; then put on a thick coating of the icing, decorate with the rest of the icing through a forcer to ornament the edges, and place the crystallised fruits on the top.

ALMOND PASTE

1 lb. of ground almonds.   4 large tablespoonfuls of
¾ lb. of icing sugar.   orange flower water.
The whites of 4 eggs.

Boil the sugar and orange flower water for six or seven minutes, then add the ground almonds. Take it away from the heat and mix in quickly the four whites of egg, one at a time. Turn out on to an oiled slab and let it cool. Afterwards roll it out the size of the cake and place it on the top, keeping it quite smooth.

Now wrap up the cake in some white paper (greaseproof) and put it away until a week before the wedding, when it may be iced and decorated.

ICING FOR WEDDING CAKE

2 lbs. of icing sugar.   The whites of 4 eggs.
Juice of 2 lemons.

Rub the icing sugar through a hair sieve: put the whites of two eggs and the juice of one lemon into a basin large enough to hold all the icing when finished, work well with a wooden spoon, adding half the sugar gradually and keeping the icing smooth; then add alternately white of egg, lemon juice and sugar, until all is in. Spread a layer all over the cake (rather a thin layer); let this dry, then put the remainder all over the cake, dipping a palette knife into cold water to keep the icing smooth. Place in a cool oven with the door wide open to dry; or leave it until the next day, when it should be covered with a transparent icing made in the following manner:

TRANSPARENT ICING

1 lb. of white sugar.   ¼ pint of cold water.

Boil for six or seven minutes: then remove from the fire and rub with a wooden spoon against the side of the pan, until it looks milky; then pour this all over the cake; let it set.

The cake is now ready to decorate, and for this purpose make an icing a little stiffer, using more sugar. This icing needs an icing forcer to form flowers and leaves or trellis work, etc., and should be made as icing for wedding cake; or there might be some over which could be used by adding just a little more sugar.

HOT CROSS BUNS

The old Bun House at Chelsea was situated at the end of Jew's Road, now called Pimlico Road, and was demolished in the year 1839. The house was sold and pulled down, but this was the original place where hot cross buns were sold as well as Chelsea buns. On Good Friday morning the Bun House presented a scene of great bustle; upon one occasion upwards of 50,000 persons having assembled there. King George II. with Queen Caroline and Princesses frequently honoured the proprietor, Mrs. Hand, with their patronage; so also did George III. and Queen Charlotte.

Recipe

1½ lbs. of flour.   ¾ pint of warm milk.
¼ lb. of butter.   2 eggs and a little spice.
1 oz. of yeast.   2 ozs. of sugar.
          ¼ lb. of currants.

George III and Queen
Charlotte

Let the butter dissolve in the milk, cream the yeast with a little of the sugar, and pour the warm milk and butter on to this. Then put the flour with the spice in a large basin, make a well in the centre and set the dough, which should rise in about one and a half hours. Then beat in the eggs, add the currants and sugar, and let it rise again. Turn out on to a board and knead, form into buns, and lay these in rows on a baking sheet, leaving 2-in. spaces between. These must now prove. When risen, mark them across and across with an ivory or bone paper knife, and bake in a quick oven ten to fifteen minutes. Brush over with milk and sugar whilst hot to glaze them as they come from the oven.

CHELSEA BUNS

¾ lb. of flour.   ½ oz. of yeast.
¼ lb. of butter.   1 lemon.
¼ lb. of sugar.   2 eggs.
                       ½ gill of milk.

Cream the yeast with a little sugar, and add to it the warm milk. Rub half the butter into the flour and add half of the sugar. Make a dough with this and beat in the eggs. Stand in a warm place to rise for about two hours. Knead well and roll out on a floured board the same way as for a jam roll, spread the rest of the butter and sugar over, fold in three, roll out again, and then into a square. Roll up as for a jam roll, cut in thick slices all the same depth and stand up on end to bake, each roll touching the other. Let them prove for about twenty minutes, then bake for the same time. The grated rind of the lemon is used for flavouring.

SHROVE TUESDAY PANCAKE

Shrove Tuesday is universally known as Pancake Day, and for hundreds of years the custom of eating pancakes on this day has been observed. Various odd ceremonies are connected with Pancake Day—for instance, at Eton and at Westminster School. When Henry VIII. founded the College of Westminster, he put the Headmaster and the Usher of the King's Scholars with the boys in the Abbey kitchen, so it was probably here that the pancake was originally tossed. It was customary in those days for the under clerk of the College to enter, preceded by the beadle and other officers, and to throw a large pancake over the bar dividing the upper and the lower school. At the present day the cook brings in the pancake and tosses it over the bar; the lucky scholar who gets it whole or the largest piece in the general scramble carries it to the Deanery and receives one guinea, the cook receives two guineas, and both are paid from the Abbey funds.

In 1919 the King and Queen were present at Westminster to see the pancake tossed and the scramble of the boys for the largest piece.

BATTER FOR PANCAKES

¾ lb. of flour.	1½ pints of milk.
3 eggs.	Pinch of salt.

Pass the flour through a sieve into a basin and add a pinch of salt; make a well in the centre and break the eggs into it with a little of the milk; mix well and keep adding more milk until all is in. It should be quite smooth and creamy. Then beat well for ten minutes, and it should stand for at least an hour before using. When ready pour into a jug. Put some lard into a small saucepan to get hot, and pour a large teaspoonful into a hot frying pan. Then pour a thin layer of the batter into the pan, and cook it gently until set and brown underneath. Then take up the pan, give it a shake and a sharp toss so as to turn the pancake over, and cook for about half a minute. Turn out on to a paper covered with castor sugar, squeeze some lemon-juice over, and fold up quickly. Proceed in the same manner for the rest of the pancakes.

Shrove Tuesday

SCOTLAND

GIRDLE SCONES

1 lb. of flour.

½ pint of buttermilk.

1 teaspoonful of bicarbonate of soda.

½ teaspoonful of tartaric acid, *or*

2 teaspoonfuls of baking powder.

1 teaspoonful of salt.

Mix the flour, raising mixture, and salt together, and pass it through a sieve into a basin. Mix quickly with the buttermilk. Turn out and knead lightly, and roll out about ¼ in. thick. Cut into rounds with a tin cutter. Lightly grease a hot girdle with butter, lay the scones on and bake quickly. When well risen and a little browned underneath, turn on the other side for a couple of minutes. If no girdle is at hand, use a thick sheet of iron.

SCOTCH SCONES

1 lb. of flour.

1 oz. of castor sugar.

3 ozs. of sultanas.

3 ozs. of butter.

½ pint of cold milk.

2 teaspoonfuls of baking powder.

Take a basin and sieve the pound of flour and baking powder together, in which rub the butter, and add the sultanas and castor sugar. Mix all well together and add the ½ pint of cold milk. Turn out on to the board and knead well. Form into two rounds and place them on a flat baking sheet, and cut each round across and across, so as to form four scones from each

…d. Brush them over with an egg, and prick them on the
…op with a fork. Bake in a quick oven from fifteen to twenty
minutes.

DUNDEE CAKE

¾ lb. of butter.   6 ozs. of mixed candied peel
¾ lb. of castor sugar.   (chopped).
10 ozs. of flour.   ¾ lb. of eggs weighed in their
½ lb. of currants.   shells.
                 Some blanched almonds.

Cream the butter and sugar, beat in half the eggs one at a
time, then sift in half the flour and add the fruit and candied
peel, then beat in the rest of the eggs one by one and then the
last of the flour. Place the mixture in a greased cake tin, spread
flat and cover with almonds. Dust a little castor sugar over and
bake in a moderate oven. When done, as soon as the cake comes
out of the oven, brush it over with a little orange syrup, and let
it dry and cool.

SCOTCH PICKLED HAMS (UNSMOKED)

2 hams (moderate size).   ½ lb. of bay salt.
2 lbs. of brown sugar.   ¼ lb. of sal prunella.
3 lbs. of salt.   1 pint of old ale.

Place the hams in a pickling pan and rub in all the ingredients,
mixing them thoroughly first. Turn and rub the hams every
morning for a fortnight. Then hang them up to dry in an airy
place and use when required.

PORRIDGE

Porridge is an immensely popular dish, and is made from
oats, the coarse oatmeal is usually employed to make the
porridge. It is well to make it in a double saucepan, filling the
lower with boiling water. The general proportion is 1 oz.

or one tablespoonful of oatmeal to ½ pint of water. Sprinkle the oatmeal into boiling water and stir with a wooden spoon, taking care to prevent the porridge becoming lumpy—this will take one hour—or boiling water may be poured on the oatmeal overnight, and then cook for about twenty minutes in the morning. Salt to taste is added ten minutes before the porridge is cooked, never at the commencement. Another plan, and quite a good one, is to bring the porridge to the boil, and to continue the cooking during the night in a hay box. This can be made with a biscuit box and a nest of hay inside. Put the vessel containing the porridge, with a tight-fitting lid, into this nest, cover with some more hay—it must all be tightly packed—replace the lid of the biscuit box, and in the morning the porridge will be nearly hot enough to serve, and quite free from lumps. Serve with milk or buttermilk and cream in small porridge plates, and salt.

FLUMMERY

This is another oatmeal dish which is very popular in the North.

To make it, put 4 ozs. of oatmeal in a white pudding basin and pour a quart of cold water over it. Place it on a corner of the kitchener, or the hob of an open fire, and stir it occasionally. When it tastes rather sour, boil it up like porridge, and serve it either with cream or milk.

WHOLEMEAL SCONES

1 lb. of whole meal.	2 teaspoonfuls of cream of tartar.
1 teaspoonful of bicarbonate of soda.	1 oz. of castor sugar.
3 ozs. of butter.	½ pint of milk.

Rub the butter into the meal, then mix the soda, cream of tartar, and sugar together, and mingle all well in the basin,

an immensely popular dish

mixing it into a stiff dough with the milk. Form into two rounds, and cut each round across and across into four. Bake on a greased baking sheet about twenty minutes, and brush over with a little milk when half baked.

SCOTCH OAT CAKES

1 lb. of oatmeal.	1 teaspoonful of salt.
1 oz. of butter or lard.	A pinch of bicarbonate of soda.

Rub the butter into the oatmeal, add the salt and the soda. Then mix into a stiff paste with boiling water. Turn on to a pastry board and roll out very thinly, cut into oval shapes, and bake on a girdle on one side only. The other side should be toasted before a fire when required for the table.

PETTICOAT TAILS

The right name is really " petits gatelles," but in the east of Scotland these cakes take the name of " Petticoat Tails "; the pronunciation being somewhat similar. To make them, the ordinary shortbread is formed into a round, cut across into eight or ten triangular pieces, dusted over with castor sugar, and then very slowly baked.

HAGGIS

1 sheep's head and loin.	½ lb. of oatmeal.
1 lb. of suet.	Salt and pepper to taste,
1 lb. of onions.	and a little spice.

The national dish of Scotland, spoken of by Burns as " great chieftain of the pudding race," and used at all great festivities, is made by taking the stomach of a freshly killed animal and filling it with vegetables, oatmeal, liver, and sometimes steak, and boiling it in this natural cover instead of in a pudding cloth. By using the stomach whilst it is still fresh, the digestive glands are still active. Consequently haggis is easily digested and nourishing. Haggis really came from the Abruzzi in Italy, and it was introduced into Scotland by the Romans, whose custom it was to use soldiers who came from the hills to occupy a hilly country.

Well clean the haggis bag and boil the sheep's head and liver, chop it up finely, shred the suet, chop the onions finely, add the oatmeal, season well, and put the mixture in the haggis bag—it should be about half full—put it into about 1 pint of the liquor the sheep's head was boiled in, and sew up the bag, pressing out the air. Then boil it gently for three or four hours, and prick it occasionally with a needle to prevent its bursting.

HOTCH POTCH

A breast of mutton or lamb.	2 young onions.
2 carrots.	2 leaves of celery.
2 turnips.	1 quart of shelled peas.

Pepper and salt.

Cut up the meat into small dice, put it into 2 quarts of cold water and let it come to the boil, skim well, then add the carrots, onions, turnips, and celery, also cut in quite small dice. Cook very slowly for six hours, then add the peas half an hour before serving. Any vegetables in season may be used in hotch potch to make a variety.

NATIONAL BUN LOAF
(Scotch Currant Bun)

2 ozs. of currants.	2 teaspoonfuls of baking powder and cinnamon.
2 ozs. of raisins.	
2 ozs. of orange peel.	1 teaspoonful of ground ginger.
4 ozs. of blanched almonds.	1 teaspoonful of allspice.
$\frac{3}{4}$ lb. of flour.	1 grated nutmeg.
$\frac{3}{4}$ lb. of sugar.	1 teacupful of milk.

introduced into Scotland by the Romans

Mix all the dry ingredients, then add the milk and mix well, and put it into a tin prepared in the following manner; giving it a good dapping to make it stick together.

THE PASTE FOR THE BUN

2 ozs. of flour.   1 oz. of butter.

Rub the butter into the flour and mix with water to a stiff paste. Roll out until very thin; butter the tin, and line the bottom and sides of the tin with the paste. Pack the bun mixture in, wet the edges. Cut a round piece of pastry for the top, cover it and join edges. Press it as flat as possible and brush it over with beaten egg, then prick it over with a fork and bake in a moderate oven.

COCK-A-LEEKIE

(An old Scotch Recipe)

1 old fowl.   ½ lb. of prunes.
4 lbs. of shin of beef.   1 teaspoonful of pepper.
3 dozen leeks.   2 teaspoonfuls of salt.
4 quarts of cold water.

Truss the fowl as for boiling, cut up the beef in small pieces. Soak the leeks, wash them well and cut in thin slices, using as much of the green ends as possible. Put all into a large pot, except the prunes. Boil gently for four hours, then add the prunes and boil for one hour longer. Take up the fowl and cut up the best parts in small pieces and return it to the soup, and leave the best pieces of the beef also, removing just the stringy and sinewy pieces. The prunes should be left in the soup.

MUFFINS

1 pint of warm milk.   2 lbs. of flour.
¼ pint of brewer's yeast.   1 egg, and a little salt.
1 oz. of butter.

Muffins

Mix all these ingredients well together and beat up well with the hand. Set the mixture to rise. Make the muffins round, using a little extra flour to keep the dough from sticking, let them remain a few minutes, and then bake them on an iron or steel plate.

CRUMPET

Use the same mixture, but only half the quantity of flour Beat it well and let it rise until bubbles are formed on the top, then bake in small polished iron tins with a little rim, on the top of an iron baking sheet.

Muffins and crumpets may be cooked in a frying pan with a moderate heat underneath. Turning them when slightly browned.

SCOTCH PIKELETS

Use the same mixture as for crumpets, with the addition of two eggs well beaten in. Put about a dessertspoonful on to a hot girdle and let it spread itself out so that it is quite thin. When lightly browned underneath, turn it with a palette knife and cook the other side. Pikelets should be served hot and well buttered.

ABERDEEN FINNAN HADDIES

Findhorn, near Aberdeen, is famous for these haddocks; they are the ordinary fish cured and dried at this fishing village, which holds a high reputation for its method. The original of the smoked and cured haddock is as follows: A fire broke out in one of the fish-curing houses, and when the flames were extinguished, the Maister pulled out one hot haddock, smelt it, and then tasted it, then ate another piece, and then another, remarking as he did so, " It's nae so nasty; taste it you, Sandy?" Then all the fishermen living in the place came to taste the haddocks, for the news spread quickly. From that time this little village, and now the greater fishing village of Findon a mile away, always cure the haddocks by smoking them over burning seaweed. The haddock tradition ascribes the dark spot on either side of the body to the impression of the thumb and finger of St. Peter; this being the species of fish in which was found the tribute money.

Scotch Method of Cooking Haddocks

If the dried haddock should be very salt, soak them in water overnight. To cook them for breakfast, lay them in a shallow tin with one bay leaf, cover them with milk and water in equal parts, and let them cook gently until done through. Then take up the haddocks, let them drain, and serve on a hot dish with morsels of butter on the top and a sprinkling of pepper over them.

AYRSHIRE ROLLED BACON

1 small side of home fed pork.	½ lb. of brown sugar.
1 oz. of saltpetre.	6 ozs. of salt.

1 pint of white vinegar.

Bone the pork first of all, then mix the salt, sugar, and saltpetre together, and rub this well into the pork, especially on the cut side where the bones have been removed. Put it in a dry pickling pan and leave it for three days. Then pour in the vinegar, and turn the pork every day for a month. Take it up and let it drain for twenty-four hours, flatten it out, and then roll it up tightly, the rind outwards, and fasten with some strong string. Hang it up in a current of air until it is quite dry. This bacon may be boiled and served cold, or cut in slices and fried or grilled in the ordinary way.

in a current of air

AYRSHIRE SHORTBREAD

¼ lb. of flour.	2 ozs. of castor sugar.
¼ lb. of rice flour.	1 egg.
¼ lb. of butter.	1 tablespoonful of cream

Mix the two flours together in a basin, rub the butter in till it is fine like crumbs, then add the sugar. Make a well in the centre, drop in the egg and cream, make into a paste, turn on to the board and knead until quite smooth. Roll out about ¾ in. thick, and cut out rounds with a cutter. Bake on a buttered paper on a baking sheet from ten minutes to a quarter of an hour. Dust well with castor sugar when taken from the oven, and let them stay on the baking sheet for a while, then lift them on to a sieve to cool.

ATHOLE CAKES

¼ lb. of maize meal.	1 heaped teaspoonful of baking
2 ozs. of castor sugar.	powder.
6 ozs. of butter.	1 lemon, and a little peel
2 eggs.	(candied).

Mix the maize meal, sugar, and baking powder together; shred the candied peel, and grate the lemon peel. In another basin beat the butter to a cream, then mix in one egg, and after that half of the dry ingredients; then add the second egg and the rest of the meal, etc. Grease some patty pans and fill them half full with the mixture and bake for about six minutes. The patty pans must be quite small ones.

SCOTCH PANCAKES

3 ozs. of flour.	About 3 drops of lemon and
3 tablespoonfuls of milk.	vanilla essence.
3 eggs.	1 teaspoonful of sugar.
½ pint of cream.	A pinch of salt.

Mix the flour and milk to a smooth paste, add the yolks of the three eggs one at a time, then the cream and flavouring, and let the batter stand to cool for awhile. When ready to fry; whip up the whites of the eggs to a strong froth and mingle them into the batter thoroughly. Fry in the usual way to commence, but when ready to toss, do not turn them; brown the upper part with a salamander or under a gas griller, Put a little warm jam or marmalade on each and roll them up, sprinkling with castor sugar.

EDINBURGH SHORTBREAD

¾ lb. of flour.	½ lb. of butter.
¼ lb. of rice flour.	¼ lb. of castor sugar.

Mix the flour and castor sugar together, and knead the butter well in. Turn on to a board and continue kneading until quite smooth and free from cracks. Roll out and form into round or square cakes as desired, crimping the edges and pricking the centres. Strips of candied peel and white carraway comfits may be used for decoration if desired. Bake on a greased paper on baking sheets in a very steady oven from three-quarters to one hour. Allow to cool before removing from tin. Dust over with castor sugar.

Scotch people send shortbread to their friends in token of remembrance.

ABERNETHY BISCUITS

1 oz. of butter.	⅜ oz. of carraway seeds.
1 lb. of the finest flour.	2 eggs.
½ oz. of sugar.	A little milk.

Rub the butter into the flour, then add the sugar and carraway seeds and mix with the eggs and milk. Knead it well and roll out and shape into round cakes. This quantity will make about eight or ten biscuits. Prick them well with a fork, right through to the baking sheet, and bake slowly in a moderate oven.

ELCHO SCONES

¾ lb. of flour.
3 ozs. of butter.
½ teaspoonful of baking powder.

1 egg.
¼ pint of buttermilk.
A pinch of salt.

Sift the flour and baking powder, rub in the butter until it forms small crumbs, make a well in the centre, drop in the egg, add the buttermilk, and form into a light dough. Do this quickly with a broad-bladed knife, then knead for a minute. Divide into three pieces and form each into a round with the hands, about 1 in. thick. Bake on a greased tin, making each one in four with a wooden spatula, and prick all over the top with a fork. Bake about twenty minutes and brush over with milk, when cooked. Then divide into four and serve.

PITCAITHLEY BANNOCK

1 lb. of flour, well dried.
½ lb. of butter.
2 ozs. of sugar.

2 ozs. of almonds, blanched and sliced thinly.
2 ozs. of candied orange peel, finely chopped.

Mix the flour and sugar, almonds, and orange peel together on a pastry board. Put the butter in the centre, and knead it together until all is well blended. Roll out and form into round cakes, pinch the edges, and prick the centre with a fork. Bake on a greased paper on a baking sheet in a moderate oven, for one hour.

with a wooden spatula

KIRKCUDBRIGHT: SCOTCH BROTH

1½ lbs. of scrag end of mutton.   1 dessertspoonful of brown
3 onions.   sugar.
1 cabbage.   2 carrots.
½ lb. of pearl barley.   Pepper and salt to taste.

Put on 3 quarts of water to boil, slice the cabbage, chop the onions and carrots finely, put all the ingredients into the water and let all simmer together for three and a half hours; then serve. This broth is very often served for shooting lunches; if well wrapped in a soup tureen and covered with flannel, it will keep hot for an hour or two.

RUTHVEN CAKE

14 ozs. of flour.   1½ large tablespoonfuls of
3 ozs. of castor sugar.   brewer's yeast or ½ oz. of
¼ lb. of fresh butter.   compressed yeast.
2 eggs.   Rind of a lemon.
1½ pints of milk.   A little powdered cinnamon.

Warm the butter and milk together until the butter is quite dissolved. Let it get lukewarm, and then mix it with the yeast. In a large basin put the flour, well dried and sifted, and in it mix the castor sugar, the lemon rind (finely minced), and a pinch of powdered cinnamon. Pour the yeast and milk on to this and next stir in the eggs, which must be well beaten up first. Set to rise for two hours, and when well risen, knead the dough for a few minutes, then put it into a buttered tin which must be only half filled with the cake mixture. Let it prove, in the same way as for bread, and then bake in a well-heated oven for about an hour.

MUTTON HAM

A shoulder of mutton.
2 ozs. of bay salt.
$\frac{1}{2}$ lb. of common salt.
$\frac{1}{4}$ lb. of brown sugar.

$\frac{1}{2}$ oz. of saltpetre.
2 ozs. of black pepper and
some juniper berries.

Mutton hams are very popular in the Highlands as a breakfast dish. The shoulders of mutton are pickled in the following manner.

Pound all the ingredients together, make them hot, and rub about half into the mutton. After two days make the other half hot and rub that in. Turn the meat every day for a fortnight. It should then be smoked, and will keep well for three or four months. Soak before boiling for two hours, and then cook as for a ham, in the usual way.

very popular in
the Highlands

WALES

THE LEEK

THE leek has been known from the remotest times, and according to ancient historians was included amongst the luxuries of the Egyptians. The Scotch are very fond of it in their cocky-leeky soup; but it is the Welsh who have it for their badge. When the Welsh won the battle over the Saxons on March 1, 640, they put leeks into their hats to distinguish themselves from their enemies, by the order of St. David; and all patriotic Welshmen have ever since followed on St. David's day (March 1), the custom of wearing the leek in memory of the victory. In South Wales, when labourers attend to plough the land of a small farmer, it is customary for each one to bring some leeks, with which a soup is made for them by the farmer's wife.

LEEK PORRIDGE

Wash, scald, and skin the leeks, then put them into sufficient fresh water to cover them, then season with salt and pepper. Stew them gently until tender, then cut in very thin slices. Make hot on some of the liquor in which they were stewed, serve in porridge or soup plates, and hand toast cut into finger pieces.

LAVER

This is a seaweed growing on the South Wales coast, where it is much used as a vegetable. It requires at least three or four hours cooking in salted water. When done, drain well and chop finely. Then make a tablespoonful of butter hot in the saucepan, put in the laver, add a squeeze of lemon juice, and serve on hot buttered toast.

The luxuries of the Egyptians

BOILED DUCK (SALTED)

1 duck.
Some large onions.

Milk.
Pepper and salt.

Salt the duck the day previously, then put it in a saucepan
with cold water sufficient to cover and let it come to the boil,
removing the scum as it rises. Simmer very gently for an hour
and a quarter. Dish up and pour some onion sauce over.

ONION SAUCE

1 lb. of onions.
½ pint of melted butter.

5 white peppercorns.
Salt.

Boil the onions in water until tender and pass them through
a sieve; make ½ pint melted butter sauce, adding peppercorns
and salt; then add the onions. Mix them well with the sauce
and serve very hot.
This is an old Welsh dish.

WELSH RAREBIT

4 ozs. of cheese.
2 large tablespoonfuls of ale.
2 slices of toast (about ½ in.
thick).
Pepper, salt, and mustard to taste.

Put the ale into a small saucepan and add to it the cheese
cut in thin flakes, and let it melt. Season with pepper, salt,
and a little mustard, and put in 1 oz. of butter. When
thoroughly hot, pour this mixture on the hot toast, just brown
it under the grill, then serve immediately.

put leeks in their hats

HUISH CAKES

¼ lb. of ground rice.
¼ lb. of flour.
½ lb. of sifted sugar.

¼ lb. of butter.
4 eggs.
A few carraway seeds, if liked.

Mix the butter and sugar to a cream, add the flour and ground rice, and lastly the whites of eggs beaten to a stiff froth.
When well mixed add the yolks (well beaten).
Stir well until all is mingled.
Place in well-greased cake tin, and bake for one hour.

WELSH PIKELETS

½ lb. of flour.
2 ozs. of castor sugar.
A pinch of salt.

1 teaspoonful of bicarbonate of soda.
¼ lb. of buttermilk.

Put flour and sugar into a basin and mix gradually into a thick batter with the buttermilk. Dissolve the bicarbonate of soda in ½ gill of boiling water and add to the mixture last. Take a tablespoonful of this batter and fry in a little hot lard, the same as in frying pancakes, and turn when half cooked with a flat-bladed knife. To be eaten hot and well buttered.

WELSH CHEESECAKES

1 egg, and the same weight in flour, butter, and sugar.

Some grated lemon rind.
Flaky pastry.

Cream the butter and sugar together, then mix in the egg and last of all the flour and the lemon rind. Line some patty pans with the pastry and put about a dessertspoonful in the centre of each patty pan, and bake.

WELSH SPICED BEEF

10 or 12 lbs. of silverside of beef.	2 ozs. of allspice.
2 ozs. of saltpetre.	2 ozs. of black pepper.

¼ lb. of salt.

Rub the saltpetre well into the fresh beef, and put by for twenty-four hours; then rub in all the other ingredients well mixed together. Place the beef in an earthenware pan, and let it remain in this pickle for a fortnight, turning it every day. Fillet with tape and put it into a clean pan to bake, pour some melted suet over it and then cover the top of the pan with a plain crust of flour and water; bake in a very slow oven for twelve hours. It may be put in the kitchener oven in the evening, and taken out the next morning. Take the crust off the top; then place the meat between two flat dishes and press with a weight on the top. This beef should be eaten cold, and will be quite nice and fresh for some time, especially in the winter months.

BARA-BRITH
The National Bun Loaf of Wales

½ lb. of raisins.	2 ozs. of candied peel.
½ lb. of currants.	½ oz. of mixed spice.
½ lb. of sultanas.	¾ oz. of yeast.
½ lb. of sugar.	¾ pint of hot water.
½ lb. of lard.	¾ pint of milk.
3 lbs. of flour.	3 eggs.

Make a dough in the usual way with the flour, water, milk, and yeast; let it rise well. When ready, melt the lard, making it just lukewarm, and beat this in, then gradually add the fruit, which must be well cleaned and picked over; add the candied peel very finely shredded, then the spice, and lastly beat in the eggs. When all is very thoroughly mixed, form into two equal pieces, knead each thoroughly and put into ordinary bread tins. Let the loaves stand to rise for half an hour in a warm place, then bake in a hot oven for about an hour.

The National Bun

IRELAND

PIG'S FACE

THIS dish is always in evidence at a national dinner, and corresponds in that way with the Scotch haggis.

Half a pig's head.   Cabbage.

Singe off all the hair and put the cheek to steep in sufficient cold water to cover it, for about twelve hours. Wash it thoroughly, especially the ear, etc. Put it on to boil in a saucepan full of cold water; no salt is to be used. Skim well as it comes to boiling point, and then let it simmer gently, allowing twenty-five minutes for each pound in weight. When done, take up the cheek, lay it on a tin, closely score the skin, and toast it a golden brown under the griller or before the fire. Cabbage should serve as a garnish round the dish.

The liquor should be saved, and may be used as a foundation for lentil or pea soup.

IRISH HUNTER'S PIE

Neck of mutton.   Pepper and salt.
2 dozen potatoes.   Gravy.

Take the best part of a neck of mutton, and cut it into neat chops, and braise them for half an hour. Boil and mash the potatoes and season them. Butter a large pie dish, line it with the potatoes, put in the chops, cover with the rest of the potatoes, and bake for half an hour. Then cut a hole in the centre and fill up with some good hot gravy.

singe off all the hair

IRISH BARN BREAK

¼ quartern of dough.   4 eggs.
6 ozs. of sugar.   2 ozs. of carraway seeds.
                          ¼ lb. of butter.

Melt the butter, beat it into the dough with the sugar, then beat in the eggs one at a time, and lastly the carraway seeds. Make this into a round loaf, or put it in a large cake tin and let it rise, then bake about forty minutes.

IRISH STEW

2 lbs. of scrag end of neck of   1 lb. of onions.
   mutton.   Black pepper and salt.
3 lbs. of potatoes.   ½ pint of water.

Cut the meat into neat pieces, peel and slice the potatoes and the onions, and place in a thick saucepan first a layer of meat, then potatoes, and then onions, sprinkling pepper and salt over each; then another layer of meat, potatoes, and onions, and so on. Add the ½ pint of cold water; let it come slowly to the boil, remove the scum, and gently simmer for three hours The vegetables should be cooked to quite a pulp.

IRISH OR CARRAGEEN MOSS MOULD

½ oz. of moss.   2 strips of lemon rind.
1 pint of milk or water.   1 teaspoonful of sugar.

Well wash and soak the moss in cold water; put the milk with the sugar and lemon rind on to simmer for ten minutes; strain the milk on to the moss, and boil for half an hour; strain. When cold it will set to a jelly. If required as an invalid beverage, double the amount of milk can be added.

POTATOES

The Irish people always boil the potatoes in their jackets, which gives them a very much better flavour.

Take a small knife and cut away about ½ inch of peel right round the centre of the potato before boiling, and when they are done the potato skins can easily be removed with one pull at either end.

IRISH POTATO CAKE

6 good white boiled potatoes.	Flour.
Salt.	Butter.

Mash potatoes till they are of a creamy consistency, adding salt, and then sufficient flour to make dough thick enough to roll. Roll out to a ½-in. thickness, cut into rectangular pieces, and bake on a griddle. Split and butter immediately, and serve very hot.

POTATO PANCAKES

2 lbs. of potatoes.	2 tablespoonfuls of flour.
1 large onion.	1 egg.

Pepper and salt to season.

Wash, peel, and grate the potatoes, put them in a cloth and squeeze out all the water. Chop the onion very finely and add to the potato, with the flour, pepper and salt. Beat up the egg, stir it well in, and make up into small round cakes, fry these in a little lard in a frying pan, and when brown underneath, turn round the other side.

COLCANNON

2 ozs. of bacon fat.	1 onion.
1 lb. of cold boiled potatoes.	½ lb. of boiled cabbage.

A little salt and pepper.

Mash the potatoes, melt the dripping in a saucepan and fry in it the onion (peeled and chopped small), and mix with the finely chopped cabbage and the potatoes. Season with salt and pepper, mix well and re-heat. Put the mixture into a greased pudding basin, make thoroughly hot in the oven, then turn out on a dish and serve.

RINK CAKE

2 eggs.	2 ozs. of butter.
1 teaspoonful of baking powder.	2 ozs. of sweet almonds.
¼ lb. of castor sugar.	1 oz. of currants.
¼ lb. of flour.	A pinch of salt.

Clean the currants, blanch and chop the almonds, then rub the butter into the flour, add the sugar and baking powder mixed together, and form into a dough with the eggs. Bake this mixture in a well-greased shallow tin, sprinkling all the almonds and currants on the top. The cake will take about twenty minutes to bake.

IRISH PANCAKES

4 eggs.	1½ oz. of butter.
⅛ pint of cream.	3 ozs. of flour.
A little grated nutmeg and castor sugar.	

Beat up the whites of two eggs with the yolks of four and mingle them into the warm cream; melt the butter and add that, then mix into a smooth batter with the flour, and flavour with the nutmeg. Fry the pancakes, which should be very thin, using a little butter for the first one, and the others will not require any. Serve very hot and roll each in some castor sugar.

IRISH ROLLS

1 lb. of flour.
½ teaspoonful of bicarbonate of
   soda.

1 egg.
1 teaspoonful of castor sugar.
½ teaspoonful of salt.

Some buttermilk.

Beat the white of the egg to a froth; dissolve the soda in the buttermilk and mix the salt with the flour and the rest of the ingredients, using just enough buttermilk to make it up into a stiff dough. Shape into rolls, brush over with the beaten-up yolk of the egg, and place on a slightly greased baking sheet. Bake about fifteen minutes.

IRISH ROCK

½ lb. of butter.
¼ lb. of castor sugar.
¾ lb. of ground almonds.
1 oz. of bitter almonds.

1 oz. of sweet almonds.
1 wineglass of brandy.
Some green preserved fruits,
   or crystallised greengages.

Pound the ground almonds, butter, and sugar together in a mortar. Blanch the bitter almonds, chop them finely, and add lastly, the brandy, and continue pounding until the mixture is quite firm, white, and smooth. Then take two spoons, and shape into egg form and pile high on a glass dish. The ounce of sweet almonds must be blanched and cut into spikes. Garnish with these, and also the green crystallised fruit; finishing with a sprig of myrtle placed on the top of the pyramid. This dish is served as a dessert sweet.

IRISH BLACK PUDDING

½ lb. of beef suet.
¼ lb. of breadcrumbs.
¼ lb. of currants.
½ pint of cream.
2 ozs. of ground almonds.

2 ozs. of candied peel.
¼ lb. of sugar.
½ teaspoonful of mixed spice.
2 eggs.
1 tablespoonful of brandy.

a dessert sweet

Shred and chop the suet finely mix with the breadcrumbs; then add the currants picked and washed, the ground almonds, the candied peel finely chopped, sugar, and spice. Separate the yolks from the whites of the eggs, and beat the latter to a stiff froth. Mix in first the beaten yolks, the cream and brandy, and lastly the whipped whites of the eggs. Turn into a well-greased mould and steam for three hours.

IRISH GIRDLE CAKES

1 lb. of flour.   1 teaspoonful of bicarbonate
A pinch of salt.   of soda.
                    ½ pint of buttermilk.

Dissolve the bicarbonate of soda in the milk, mix the salt with the flour, and make it all into a stiff paste; roll out thin and cut into rounds. Make a girdle hot, lightly grease the top, and cook the cakes on this for six or seven minutes, turning them when half done

IRISH DELIGHT

1½ ozs of cornflower.   2 eggs.
1½ pints of milk.   A little vanilla essence.
1 dessertspoonful of castor sugar.

Mix the cornflour with a little of the milk into a smooth paste. Bring the rest of the milk to the boil, remove from the heat and pour the cornflour paste into it, stirring well. Boil for about ten minutes, add the flavouring, sugar, and beaten eggs. Pour into a shallow wet tin, and when quite cold thin out, cut in oblong blocks, dip in beaten egg, roll out in bread-crumbs, and fry a golden brown in deep smoking hot fat. If desired as a savoury, omit flavouring and sugar, and substitute salt, pepper, and a little grated cheese.

H

Irish Delight

INDEX

Index

TRAVEL TO THE BRITISH ISLES
WITH HIPPOCRENE

COMPANION GUIDE TO BRITAIN: ENGLAND, SCOTLAND AND WALES
by Henry Weisser

Highlights are cited and explained: cathedrals, stately homes, villages and towns. This essential guide lists history, geography, politics, culture, economics, climate and language use.
318 pages, 6 1/2 x 8 1/4, 16 pages b/w photos, index
0-7818-0147-8 $14.95pb

LANGUAGE AND TRAVEL GUIDE TO BRITAIN
by Catherine McCormick

Let Catherine McCormick introduce you to Britain, a country of tradition, royalty and five o'clock tea. She addresses everything you need to know about planning a trip to Britain, from history, to culture, to language.
266 pages, 5 1/2 x 8 1/2, maps, photos, index
0-7818-0166 $14.95pb

COMPANION GUIDE TO IRELAND
2nd edition
by Henry Weisser
The author describes the major attractions, provides information on food, accommodations, transportation and language.
300 pages, 5 ½ x 8 1/2, b/w photos, maps, charts
0-7818-0170-2 $14.95pb

HIPPOCRENE LANGUAGE AND TRAVEL GUIDES

These guides provide an excellent introduction to a foreign country for the traveler who wants to meet and communicate with people as well as sightsee. Each book is also an ideal refresher course for anyone wishing to brush up on their language skills.

LANGUAGE AND TRAVEL GUIDE TO AUSTRALIA, by Helen Jonsen
Travel with or without your family through the land of "OZ" on your own terms; this guide describes climates, seasons, different cities, coasts, countrysides, rainforests, and the Outback with a special consideration to culture and language.
250 pages • $14.95 • 0-7818-0166-4 (0086)

LANGUAGE AND TRAVEL GUIDE TO FRANCE, by Elaine Klein
Specifically tailored to the language and travel needs of Americans visiting France, this book also serves as an introduction to the culture. Learn the etiquette of ordering in a restaurant, going through customs, and asking for directions.
320 pages • $14.95 • 0-7818-0080-3 (0386)

LANGUAGE AND TRAVEL GUIDE TO INDONESIA (Coming soon)
350 pages • $14.95 • 0-7818-0328-4 (0111)

LANGUAGE AND TRAVEL GUIDE TO MEXICO, by Ila Warner
Explaining exactly what to expect of hotels, transportation, shopping, and food, this guide provides the essential Spanish phrases, as well as describing appropriate gestures, and offering cultural comments.
224 pages • $14.95 • 0-87052-622-7 (503)

LANGUAGE AND TRAVEL GUIDE TO RUSSIA, by Victorya Andreyeva and Margarita Zubkus
Allow Russian natives to introduce you to the system they know so well. You'll be properly advised on such topics as food, transportation, the infamous Russian bath house, socializing, and sightseeing. Then, use the guide's handy language sections to be both independent and knowledgeable.
293 pages • $14.95 • 0-7818-0047-1 (0321)

LANGUAGE AND TRAVEL GUIDE TO UKRAINE, by Linda Hodges and George Chumak
Written jointly by a native Ukrainian and an American journalist, this guide details the culture, the people, and the highlights of the Ukrainian experience, with a convenient (romanized) guide to the essentials of Ukrainian.
266 pages • $14.95 • 0-7818-0135-4 (0057)

HIPPOCRENE DICTIONARY AND PHRASEBOOK SERIES

Each of these titles combines the best elements from a dictionary with the best elements of a phrasebook. Slim enough to fit in a pocket, each of these titles provides the reader with a brief grammar instruction, a 1500 word list—complete with pronunciation—and a collection of helpful phrases in many and varied topics. Conversion charts and abbreviated menus can also be found in many of the titles.

BRITISH-AMERICAN/ AMERICAN-BRITISH

Catherine McCormick
160 pages, 3 3/4 x 7
0-7818-0450-7
$11.95pb (247)

IRISH-ENGLISH/ ENGLISH-IRISH

160 pgs, 3 3/4 x 7
0-87052-110-1
$7.95pb (385)

PILIPINO-ENGLISH/ ENGLISH-PILIPINO

Raymond Barrager and Jesusa V. Salvador
192 pgs, 3 3/4 x 7
0-7818-0451-5
$8.95pb (295)

Coming Soon . . .

CHECHEN-ENGLISH/ ENGLISH-CHECHEN

Nicholas Awde
160 pgs, 3 3/4 x 7
0-7818-0446-9
$11.95pb (183)

LINGALA-ENGLISH/ ENGLISH-LINGALA

Thomas Anrwi-Akowuah
120 pgs, 3 3/4 x 7
0-7818-0456-6
$9.95pb (296)

Love Poetry from the Gaelic Tradition

IRISH LOVE POEMS
edited by Paula Redes

A beautifully illustrated anthology that offers an intriguing glimpse into the world of Irish passion, often fraught simultaneously with both love and violence. For some contemporary poets this will be their first appearance in a U.S. anthology. Included are poets Thomas Moore, Padraic Pearse, W.B.Yeats, John Montague and Nuala Ni Dhomnaill.

Gabriel Rosenstock, famous poet and translator, forwards the book, wittily introducing the reader to both the collection and the rich Irish poetic tradition.

illustrated, 176 pages, 6 x 9, 0-7818-0396-9 $14.95pb

SCOTTISH LOVE POEMS
A Personal Anthology
edited by Lady Antonia Fraser, re-issued edition

Lady Antonia Fraser has selected her favorite poets from Robert Burns to Aileen Campbell Nye and placed them together in a tender anthology of romance. Famous for her own literary talents, her critical writer's eye has allowed her to collect the best loves and passions of her fellow Scots into a book that will find a way to touch everyone's heart.

220 pages, 5 1/2 x 8 1/4, 0-7818-0406-X $14.95pb

Self-Taught Audio Language Course

Hippocrene Books is pleased to recommend Audio-Forum self-taught language courses. They match up very closely with the languages offered in Hippocrene dictionaries and offer a flexible, economical and thorough program of language learning.

Audio-Forum audio-cassette/book courses, recorded by native speakers, offer the convenience of a private tutor, enabling the learner to progress at his or her own pace. They are also ideal for brushing up on language skills that may not have been used in years. In as little as 25 minutes a day — even while driving, exercising, or doing something else — it's possible to develop a spoken fluency.

Scots Gaelic Self-Taught Language Course

Gaelic Made Easy
4 cassettes (4 hr.), 4 booklets, $69.95.
Order #HSG20.

All Audio-Forum courses are fully guaranteed and may be returned within 30 days for a full refund if you're not completely satisfied.

You may order directly from Audio-Forum by calling toll-free 1-800-243-1234.

For a complete course description and catalog of 264 courses in 91 languages, contact Audio-Forum, Dept. SE5, 96 Broad St., Guilford, CT 06437. Toll-free phone 1-800-243-1234. Fax 203-453-9774.